GREATEST MOMENTS IN
PENN STATE
FOOTBALL HISTORY

EDITED BY FRANCIS J. FITZGERALD

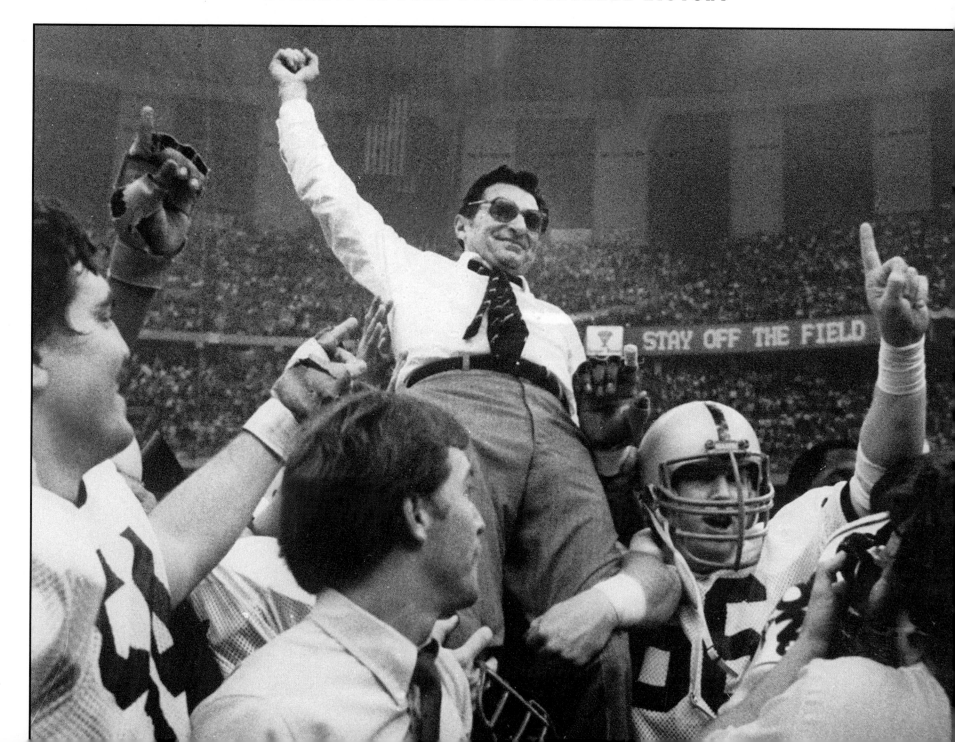

STAY OFF THE FIELD

PHOTO CREDITS

Allsport USA: 167-left.

AP/Wide World Photo: Front Cover, ii-top, ii-right, iii, iv-top left, v, 47, 54, 73, 75, 94-bottom, 111, 112-left, 115, 125, 126, 127, 129, 141, 144-both, 147,   151, 152, 157, 158, 159, 161, 162-163, 169, 170-top, 173, 174, 179, 182-both.

College Football Hall of Fame: 14-left, 28.

Cotton Bowl: 91-top, 105-both.

Orange Bowl: 93, 95.

Partee Library Archives, Penn State University: ii-bottom, iv-bottom left, iv-top right, 23, 31, 43, 48, 49-both, 52-53, 56-both, 57-both, 66, 70-71, 74, 77, 78-both, 79-both, 81, 82-top left, 83-all, 85, 86, 87, 91-bottom, 94-top, 97, 99, 109, 143, 177, 178, 184-left.

Penn State University Athletic Department: iv-bottom right, 8, 11, 12, 13, 14-right, 16-17, 18, 20-21, 24, 25, 27, 32, 35, 36, 37, 38, 41-both, 45, 51, 53, 59,   60, 63, 64, 65-both, 69, 82-bottom right, 98, 100-right, 101-all, 108, 134-right, 165, 170-bottom, 171, 181-bottom.

Pittsburgh Post-Gazette: 107, 112-right, 113, 119, 120, 121-both, 133, 134-left, 135, 148, 149, 153, 154, 166, 167-top, 180.

University of Pittsburgh Sports Information: 123.

UPI/Corbis-Bettmann Archives: 89, 90, 100-top, 100-bottom left, 103, 104, 116, 130, 131, 137, 138, 145, 181-top, 183, 184-top right, 184-bottom right.

Cover and Book Design: Lori Smith Design, Birmingham, Ala.
Published by: Epic Sports, Birmingham, Ala.

CONTENTS

THE EARLY YEARS

THE RIP ENGLE ERA

THE JOE PATERNO ERA

THE EARLY YEARS

The man who makes the Cotton Bowl trophies went back to work today with a rush order on his hands. He had to hammer out an extra copy. One will go to Penn State and the other to Southern Methodist to symbolize the 13-13 tie they played here before some 47,000 assorted and well-refrigerated Texans and Pennsylvanians, who carried virtually every hotel blanket in town to the stadium to fend off the chilly wind that whistled down from the north.

Chester L. Smith

The Pittsburgh Press

Penn State 20 Pittsburgh 0

November 27, 1919 | Pittsburgh, Pa.

Nittany Lions Feast on Panthers at Muddy Forbes Field

Penn State	7	6	7	0 —	20
Pittsburgh	0	0	0	0 —	0

For more Thanksgiving Days than they like to recall, the Mountain Lions of Penn State have advanced upon the Forbes Field salient in an effort to win a square meal and have retired, baffled and hungry, to their Mt. Nittany den to hole up for the winter … while Pitt was left in victorious possession of the field — and the turkey.

But today after six disappointments, hungers and heartaches, the Mountain Lions feasted sumptuously upon Panther meat — and picked their teeth with the shinbones of a Warner eleven. Their appetite appeased by a 20-0 score, the Blue and White warriors and fans bid the Pitt fans a polite farewell and withdrew to their mountain fortress with Jimmy DeHart's football in their possession — the first Pitt football they've lifted since 1912.

Only once, and that was near the end of the game, with the ball in Pitt's territory, did Pitt rip off one of its advances and make three successive first downs in their old-style form.

To the writer it looks as if it will be impossible to escape rating Pennsylvania State College at the top of the heap in the East this fall. The way it smothered Pitt demonstrates conclusively that it is a team second to none — and though it has been beaten by Dartmouth — the way it overrode all other opponents, coupled with the superb power and dash of its attack and the impenetrable qualities of its defense today is evidence enough to convince us and many others.

Colonel Joe Thompson, for instance. After the game we bumped into

Pittsburgh's Forbes Field was a quagmire on Thanksgiving Day 1919, limiting both teams' offensive production. According to accounts, "The field was heavy, no doubt, and State went better in the mud than Pitt, but we can't see that it had any bearing."

him. He was not hard to draw out. "Yes, State's the best on the gridiron this fall, and that man Higgins is the best end I ever saw. He's wonderful! — a superman of the gridiron."

And there are reasons for Colonel Joe's praise. Bob Higgins sprinted 75 yards for a touchdown after receiving a forward pass that was launched behind his own goal line, and crossed the Pitt goal line the first time with a touchdown that was enough to take the starch out of any opponent. And it was the most spectacular play we've seen on any gridiron.

Poor football? Yes — but superb generalship, and the result justified the long chance and the danger, for it took the ball from State's territory back of the Pitt line, removed the menace of the Blue and Gold, and was the beginning of Pitt's downfall.

It was early in the first half. On Harold Hess' first try at punting after the kickoff the ball went straight up in the air and Pitt got it on the State 23-yard line. There Pitt's attack and a penalty incurred by State took the ball to State's 6-yard line before the Panthers were stopped. Again Hess went back to punt, standing three or four yards behind his own goal line. In a case of this kind a forward pass is preposterous — unthinkable. And, simply because it was unthinkable, it was tried. A complete surprise, it worked like a dream, like a beatific miracle. Higgins started down the field, stopped on the 25-yard mark, turned, plucked the ball out of the air, and continued.

The Pitt secondary defense was drawn close in. When Higgins caught the ball nobody was between him and the Pitt goal but Hastings, who was laying back about 50 yards. Enough Penn State blockers were downfield to ward off the startled Pitt backs, and two were ahead of Higgins when he set sail down into Hastings' territory. With two determined blockers bearing down on him, the startled Hastings succumbed almost without a struggle, and Higgins gamboled the last 50 yards in a sort of a dizzy, jazzy joy ramble, to the accompaniment of a mighty Penn State paean of rejoicing.

Now, we ask you, isn't that enough to take the starch out of any team?

Another Penn State touchdown was the result of a long ramble. It was the third score and came mighty soon after the second half began. Pie Way was the hero. Little Pie Way, about the size of a pint of hard cider liberally laced with bourbon — and about as strong.

It was after Hastings had punted and it was State's ball on the Pitt 47-yard line. On the very first play Way passed like a disembodied spirit through a seemingly solid Pitt line, materialized on the other side and strutted 53 yards for a score with no one to trouble him at all after his blockers had speared the Pitt secondary defense.

And there were some blockers, too, let us tell you. We've seen quite some blocking since Warner set up shop in these parts, but Hugo Bezdek is a great teacher of blocking, too, and it worked like a 21-jeweled watch yesterday, sweeping all before it, except on some occasions when the Lions essayed wide end runs. These the Panthers could stop in their tracks, but the short knife-like thrusts in close, through the line and just off tackle, penetrated deep into the Panther defense time and time again. The Pitt line was ripped apart, harpooned, knifed, lanced, gaffed and perforated until it resembled a mass of rags and tatters.

That second touchdown, coming in the second quarter, was the culmination of a 76-yard advance which began with a 20-yard run-back of a punt — the very last

Charley (Pie) Way scored on a 53-yard run in the third quarter for Penn State's final touchdown against Pitt.

Penn State's 1919 team finished 7-1 under Coach Hugo Bezdek (top, third from left), shutting out five opponents.

beginning with Way's 40-yard kick return to past mid-field before Tom Davies dragged him down. Robb, Hess and Way moved the ball in close, but State drew a 15-yard holding penalty that relieved the pressure and, after working the ball to the 6-yard line, Pitt smeared a passing attack and took the ball away, a notable achievement.

Soon after Penn State's last touchdown a heaven-sent break gave the Panthers a chance to score. Hastings had punted "way off to one side," and Robb couldn't get under it. He trotted over to the bounding ball and it sprang up and bit him on the ankle — that put it onside for Pitt and Frank Eckert, covering the punt, fell on it. It was Pitt's ball on Penn State's 16-yard line.

Hasting, Davies and Laughran tried, but couldn't gain enough yardage on the ground to worry Penn State. But State's anxiety caused an offside play, and that gave Pitt the ball on State's five-yard mark. Here two bucks were stopped at the line of scrimmage and two passes were savagely batted down, and Pitt's last chance went glimmering.

But, though Pitt didn't score, this break evidently held the score to it final proportions, for Pitt, outpunting Penn State, kept the ball in Penn State's territory, until well toward the end of the game. And when Penn State got the ball back again, as the result of many see-saws, took the ball back to State's territory, where it was when the game ended.

Some folks are saying that the heavy field helped Penn State. The field was heavy, no doubt, and State went better in the mud than Pitt, but we can't see that it had any bearing. Superior to Pitt in the mud, Penn State was undoubtedly superior to Pitt on a dry field. And had the footing been secure Penn State very probably would have scored other touchdowns, though it is probable that Pitt would have negotiated one or two, just to ease the sting of defeat.

play of the quarter — that downed the ball on Penn State's 44 mark. Harry Robb was the hero of that return, and Robb played an important part in the dash which followed.

There was one interlude, and only one, to State's ground attack, and it came when Pitt had apparently succeeded in checking the State smashes.

Then Conover dropped back to kick a field goal from the 37-yard line — only it wasn't a field goal. Robb, who took the ball instead of Conover, shot a forward pass to Way for a 13-yard gain that took the ball to Pitt's 10-yard line. It was a pretty stratagem — well conceived and beautifully executed, and it fooled Pitt and the assembled multitudes.

Once on the 20-yard line, Penn State was not to be denied, and, in spite of Pitt's frantic resistance, lugged that ball right over and rammed it down the Panther throats.

After this touchdown Penn State again started on a scoring march,

Glenn Killinger returned a Tech kickoff 85 yards for the Nittany Lions' first touchdown.

Halfback Joe Lightner was Killinger's battery mate in the dismantling of the Georgia Tech defense.

Penn State 28 Georgia Tech 7

Lions Defeats Georgia Tech in Gotham Grid Match

Penn State crushed Georgia Tech by a score of 28-7 this afternoon at the Polo Grounds before a crowd of 28,000 spectators. The big event of the game was a touchdown scored by Glenn Killinger of Penn State, who received a Tech kickoff in the middle of the first quarter and ran 95 yards through the baffled and bewildered Tech defense for the touchdown, tying the score and shattering his opponents' morale. For the first few minutes the battle had every indication that Tech's slashing offensive drive coupled with the puzzling shift would drive Penn State off the field.

Securing control of the ball some 50 yards from the Penn State goal the Southern attack moved forward with a fine display of speed and power in which the belligerent D.I. Barron took the leading role. One first down followed another until Barron finally fought his way across the goal line as the 500 Georgia rooters who had traveled 1,000 miles raised enough racket to last a month. Massed in the stands back of first

| Penn State | 7 | 7 | 7 | 7 | — | 28 |
| Georgia Tech | 7 | 0 | 0 | 0 | — | 7 |

base, they filled the air with a wild flutter of yellow ribbons and flowers with a vocal accompaniment that rocked the huge stadium.

But with that one big march completed, the tide swerved with a swiftness that fairly took away one's breath. Up to this point, Georgia Tech had made six first downs against none for Penn State, but on the next kickoff the ball settled lightly into the arms of Killinger, and the red deer was on his way through the golden autumn afternoon with the entire Tech team in pursuit.

Using a rare quality of speed and a puzzling, zig-zag shift, he soon worked up his way to midfield and here, surrounded by fine blocking, he came into the open with the last tackler removed and no one swift enough to even approach his dizzy speed, he raced over the goal line for

15

Glenn Killinger raced 95 yards for a touchdown in the first quarter.

a play that few are lucky enough to ever see in one of the big games — a touchdown from the kickoff. Only a great back of the Killinger type is qualified to make such a play and as he bounded into the open beyond midfield the entire stands arose to pay him tribute.

He had covered 85 yards in this startling flight without being halted along the route. This was the play that turned the Southern machine upside down and settled the issue of that battle beyond any doubt. For, after this run, Penn State's powerful, well directed assault with its shifts and passes scattered Yellow Jackets up and down the field. It was easy to see that the Southern defense was far below its strong attack, for not only was its line ripped open and driven back — but it was also forward passed into a state of delirium.

On play after play Killinger, Harry Wilson or Joe Lightner would lunge forward for big gains and through these advances added to the pressure. Penn State completed pass after pass with Tech helpless upon defense, floundering badly as the ball sailed from Killinger's hands down the field to the waiting receiver. On two occasions near the end of the game, Stan McCollum, surrounded by two or three Yellow Jackets, took the ball out of the air on long accurate passes (more than 30 yards) without even being annoyed by the hostile defenders around him. On one occasion, he had to leap for the ball while still upon a dead run, surrounded by many foes.

The hard, low-charging Penn State line did its part but it was Killinger who slaughtered Tech. His speed and power was too much for Georgia Tech as it vainly tried to drag him down without substantial gains. He was a wiggling, twisting, daring, flashing, line-breaking, broken-field running wonder — one of the big stars of the year. And with Wilson and Lightner at his side, the Penn State offense was too superior to Georgia Tech's poor defense to keep the issue even fairly close.

Penn State's 1923 Rose Bowl team, which finished 6-4-1, ended the season with three consecutive losses.

USC 14 Penn State 3

January 1, 1923 | Pasadena, Calif.

Fiesty Trojans Stop Potent Penn State in Rose Bowl

By Walter Eckersall

Special to The Pittsburgh Post

Penn State	3	0	0	0 —	3
Southern Cal	0	7	7	0 —	14

Outplayed in every department of the game, with the exception of 10 minutes of the first quarter, Penn State went down in defeat to University of Southern California, 14-3, today. It was the only defeat suffered an Eastern eleven in the three intersectional games played on the West Coast during the holidays.

The Trojans assumed the aggressive shortly after the first 10 minutes of play, during which the Lions scored a field goal. After that, Coach Elmer Henderson's team ran the Penn State ends, drove through the line and off the tackles for consistent gains. The visitors were given 15 yards and Mike Palm and Harry (Lighthorse) Wilson advanced to the Trojans' 12-yard line. The locals held and Palm made a drop kick from the 20-yard line. In the second quarter Palm punted out of bounds on his 30-yard line and USC made a successful drive to the goal line with Gordon Campbell going over after a triple pass. John Hawkins kicked the extra point. In the third quarter the Trojans again began a driving

attack and Roy Baker scored, with Hawkins adding the point-after kick.

In the final period the play was entirely in Penn State's territory and the Trojans forced the issue all the way as the game ended just as the moon was coming up.

The Trojans, well coached in all angles of offensive and defensive football by Henderson, who learned his football at Oberlin, were masters of the situation after Palm had kicked the field goal for the visitors shortly after the opening of the game. They soon solved the Lions' compact offense by having the tackles and smashing ends drive in and smashed the plays before they were well under way.

The game started off with a most peculiar play. USC lost the toss and Penn State received on the south end of the field. Hawkins drove the

19

ball over the goal line, but when it struck a post over the line it bounded back into the field of play. Palm of Penn State caught it on the bound and was downed on his own five-yard line.

Penn State tried two plays then Palm punted to Harold Galloway, who was stopped on his 42-yard line. The Trojans could gain only two yards in three attempts and then Galloway tried a forward pass. The ball hit the ground and it was the visitors' ball on their 34-yard line.

Penn State was held and Palm punted out of bounds on the Trojans' 23-yard line. The visitors held and Galloway tossed to Palm. Hayden Pythian, the Trojan end, hit Palm before he had a chance to catch the ball and Southern California was given 15 yards for interfering with a fair catch. This placed the ball on the Trojans' 40-yard line. Wilson, Johnny Patton and Barney Lentz advanced the ball to U.S.C.'s 12-yard line by driving through the Trojan line and off the tackles. Palm then dropped back and made a perfect drop kick from the 20-yard line.

An exchange of punts after the next kickoff left the ball in Penn State's possession on its 28-yard line on the first play. Palm fumbled and U.S.C. recovered on the visitors' 21-yard line as the quarter ended.

Roy Baker, Campbell and Howard Kincaid carried the ball to Penn State's 1-yard line and then fumbled. The visitors recovered the ball back of their goal line for a touchback. It was a tough break for the Trojans.

After an exchange of punts, Palm recovered one of Galloway's kicks on his 15-yard line. The Trojans then mounted a drive to score. Baker got around Calvin Frank and was stopped on Penn State's 10-yard line. A dandy Baker to Galloway pass — from a spread formation — placed the ball on Penn State's 1-yard line. Galloway dove for the ball and scooped it just before it touched the ground. On a triple pass formation, Campbell drove through center for a touchdown, and Hawkins converted the extra-point kick to give USC a 7-3 lead. The remainder of the period the game was played at midfield.

Baker got around Art Artelt for 30 yards and Campbell hit center for three more. Baker was then called upon three successive times and he

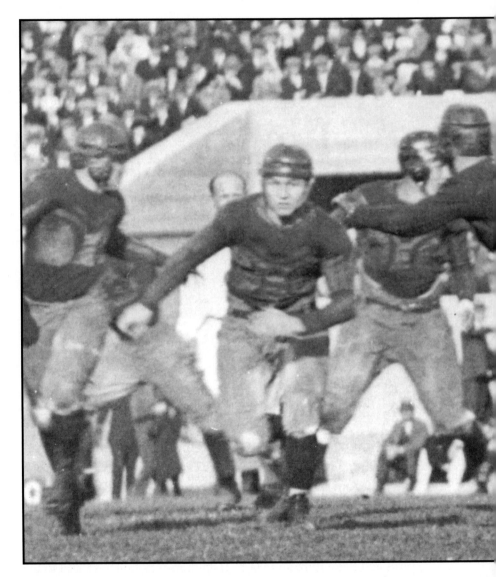

carried the ball to Penn State's one-yard line. On the next play this great back drove off Lester Logue's block for a touchdown. Hawkins again kicked the extra point to boost USC's lead to 14-3.

For the remainder of the quarter the play was in Penn State's territory. Coach Henderson finished the game with a number of substitutes.

A crowd of 43,000 at the Rose Bowl watched USC limit Penn State to a 20-yard drop kick by Mike Palm.

Most of this quarter was played in the twilight, as the game was late in starting due to an argument between the coaches over the selection of officials. The crowd was late to arrive, and it was 3 p.m. before the teams lined up for the kickoff.

USC was easily master of the game.

Penn State 13 West Virginia 13

October 27, 1923 | New York, N.Y.

West Virginia Battles Lions to a Tie at Yankee Stadium

By The Associated Press

The Pittsburgh Press

A wandering Lion of Mt. Nittany and a bold Mountaineer from West Virginia fought a terrific gridiron battle in newly built, cavernous Yankee Stadium today, and when it was over they were still undecided as to superiority, for the score was 13-all. Either team might have won by the simple twist of a kicker's toe, but fate apparently had decreed that it was to be a draw, and it was, for the extra-point kicks that might have given either side a point and victory were far wide of their marks. It was absolutely an even game from almost every angle, except that Penn State registered more first downs than West Virginia.

Both teams seemed inclined to fumble early in the game and one of these fumbles paved the way for Penn State's first touchdown five minutes after play had begun. But the same fate which had put the Lions in a position to score in this manner came to the rescue of the Mountaineers later and helped them even the count. It was the son of Mrs. Wilson — the same son who beat Navy — who kept Penn State on

Penn State	7	0	0	6 —	13
West Virginia	0	0	7	6 —	13

the map again today. It was he who registered the first touchdown; he also registered the second touchdown and booted the extra point after the first time across the Mountaineer line. But it was Dick Schuster, who made the kick that would have given Penn State a triumph. And it was Guy Ekberg's toe, the toe that had already registered one true boot between the crossbars, that failed when the time came for the kick that would have sent Fat Spears' delegation back to Morgantown with the scalp of the Nittany Lions.

Harry Wilson was the same ranting, raving, running marvel today that he has always been, though he was never able to get away for one of his famous long runs to a touchdown from a kickoff, forward pass or punt. His work today was not sensational but it was thoroughly consis-

Hugo Bezdek compiled a 65-30-11 record from 1918-1929 as Penn State's head football coach.

tent. Dashing around the ends, brushing off tackles or plunging through center, he was a grand ground-gaining maniac, good always for a fair gain, seldom stopped without some advance, but never thrown for a loss. It was he who twice plunged over the goal line and he who got away for 5, 10 and 15 yards every now and again, just when the Mountaineer defense seemed set to make a stand.

The aerial route was the Mountaineers' principal weapon of offense; in fact, it was forward passes that gave the West Virginians both their touchdowns. Once it was Nicholas Nardacci who got away with one for a touchdown, and then it was Pete Barnum.

The latter got his pass while running left end just before he had passed the line of scrimmage and eluded several Penn State tacklers to rush 18 yards for the touchdown. Nardacci's run was for about the same distance.

Penn State started as if she intended to mop up — in fact, the way her backs went through and around the Mountaineers' line in the first few minutes of the game, after the recovery of a fumble, led the 30,000 or more fans to believe they had been led to a slaughter of innocents, but the Mountaineers then began to assert themselves and fought back, holding the enemy at bay for the remainder of the first half and doing their own stuff in the second.

In the latter half, the West Virginians made the Nittany outfit look just as bad as they had been made to look in the early part of the game, and before a half dozen plays had been pulled off, the Mountaineers were on an even basis, fighting to go ahead, which they did soon after the final quarter began.

At this point, Penn State started to come back. Ray Johnston, a reserve halfback, took a punt down near his own goal line, and when they had stopped him he was well into the Mountaineers' territory.

Harry Wilson

Joe Bedenk

Then Wilson, alternating with Johnston on off-tackle smashes and end runs, carried the ball to a scant 12 or 15 yards from the goal line. From here, Wilson, almost singlehandedly, battered his way to a first down on the 1-yard line, then took a final plunge over center for the remaining distance to the goal line. Penn State fought the latter part of the battle without its captain, Joe Bedenk — who was injured and had to be helped off the field — but William House, who substituted, didn't offer the Mountaineers any encouragement, for he stopped everything that looked like a threat at his portion of the line.

Jules Prevost, a Penn State right tackle, proved himself a bearcat on both offense and defense. Twice he carried the ball, once from a kickoff and again from a partially blocked punt, and though he did not shine so brilliantly in either of his efforts, he made up for it by his deadly tackling and his ability to break through and stop plays in the making.

For the Mountaineers the lion's share of the glory went to Nardacci and Ekberg, though Jack Simons, the team captain, did some great ground-gaining at various points of the game. Ekberg's punting was off-color from the start and Barnum, who replaced Armin Mahrt, finished up as the kicker. Phil Hill, who didn't get in at the start, was trotted out soon after the beginning of the second half, and though it might have been only a coincidence, it is a fact that West Virginia perked up and scored both her touchdowns after Hill was injected into the fray.

In the handling of punts, both teams seemed to lack something, but with all the fumbling, those who saw the game were convinced at the finish that they had watched two of the East's greatest teams battle to no verdict.

Penn State 0 Notre Dame 0

November 7, 1925 | State College, Pa.

Defense, Sloppy Field are Winners as Lions Tie Notre Dame

By Knute Rockne

Special to The Pittsburgh Press

The Nittany Lions of Penn State proved themselves to be great "mud" players here today when they tied Notre Dame, 0-0. They have a tradition here that the Lions play great ball in the mud. They proved it again this afternoon.

Their defense poured in on the Notre Dame thrusts with a vengeance. They covered the Irish well on passes. Notre Dame outgained Penn State considerably, but was unable to score. Both teams had an opportunity to score a field goal, but the condition of the ball, which was heavy with mud, and the treacherousness of the footing made the two tries failures.

Notre Dame's wide sweeping runs were of no value. The Nittany Lions got to the plays before they could be formed. Both teams were fighting hard throughout, but the mud handicap proved too much of an obstacle. The Penn State offense was built close to the line and very few plays outside the tackles were tried. The most successful play Penn State

| Notre Dame | 0 | 0 | 0 | 0 — | 0 |
| Penn State | 0 | 0 | 0 | 0 — | 0 |

used was the fake off guard. This play was responsible for at least two of Penn State's three first downs. The players slipped in the mud as if they were standing on ice and forward passing was practically impossible.

A huge Homecoming crowd gathered to watch the affair. A drizzle fell throughout the game, which added to the misery of the players. Penn State tackled hard and kept their heads up throughout the encounter. Notre Dame also played smart football. A break occurred in the third quarter when Gene Edwards punted to the Penn State 1-yard line, where John Voedisch fell on the ball.

Lions captain Bas Gray, who played superb ball throughout, was forced to punt from behind his own goal line and he booted it to his own 30. The Irish started a concentrated drive which was stopped on the 9-yard line.

Penn State, in the fourth quarter, also made a determined bid for a touchdown when August Michalske made a beautiful run of 20 yards, which placed the ball on Notre Dame's 25-yard line. The Irish held, however.

The Nittany Lion attack, aimed directly over the guards and inside of the Notre Dame tackles, was powerful, well-aimed and the choice of plays was excellent. It was simply a case of a bad day slowing up both teams. What would have happened on a dry field is a question. The marvelous Penn State defensive play and the careful way in which it covered punts would have stood in good stead on any kind of a field. The players were forced to wipe the mud from their bodies throughout the game.

It was a good game to watch and both teams should be credited with great praise because of the defensive play. Gray played one of the greatest defensive games of his career.

Mike Michalske and Bill Pritchard are real backfield men. They would have shown far better if the field was dry and fast. Edwards of Notre Dame handled the team very nicely. Notre Dame's heads-up policy of following the ball was their real saving feature. Coach Hugo Bezdek revealed some clever backfield maneuvers and his team's line play was wonderful to watch. It was an even game throughout. Notre Dame outgained Penn State, both had opportunities to score a field goal, and the Irish completed three passes to one for Penn State, a short flip over the center of the line.

Halfback Johnny Roepke went on to captain the Nittany Lions' 1927 team, which finished 6-2-1.

Penn 3 Penn State 0

November 6, 1926 | Philadelphia, Pa.

Penn's Scull Boots Winning Kick Against Nittany Lions

By Ross E. Kauffman

The Pittsburgh Press

| Penn State | 0 | 0 | 0 | 0 — | 0 |
| Penn | 3 | 0 | 0 | 0 — | 3 |

Paul Scull's right foot, denied a chance at a critical time in the Illinois game a week ago, today gave Penn a 3-0 victory over Penn State on Franklin Field.

Standing on the 40-yard line in the opening period, the former Lower Marion High athlete, drop-kicked a perfect field goal as Penn's cheering section sent up a "whoop" that was heard for blocks. Before a crowd of 55,000 Scull's goal gave Penn its first victory over the Nittany Lions since 1922. Two years ago, the teams battled to a scoreless tie. There was no contest last fall.

Penn State, with a fighting team that lacked offensive drive, carried the ball within one yard of a touchdown in the second period, only to have Penn put up one of its old-time goal-line stands and take the ball over on downs.

It was a mighty close call for the Red and Blue. With the ball on the 4-yard line and first down — due to the splendid line-bucking of fullback G.R. Greene — three more yards were added on plays inside tackle.

Penn State tried to surprise Penn by tossing a short forward pass to the left side of the line. Johnny Roepke hurled the ball out toward the goal but George Delp, the former West Philadelphia High star, failed to get close to it and Penn was out of danger. After that Quaker quarterback Paul Murphy kicked from behind his own goal line and Penn State was throttled for the rest of the day.

Coach Hugo Bezdek's Lions were forever zipping forward passes but not with much success.

From a kick formation, Roepke hurled the ball right and left but could not make much headway, especially after the first half.

Paul Scull gave way to Paster Fields in the final period. The Main Line lad was pretty badly used up. The Red and Blue cheering section

28

George Delp, a Penn State end in 1926-28.

cheered him to the echo as he walked to the dressing room.

On the last play of the game, Penn's Charley Rogers, who played a remarkable game, was injured and had to be led to the sidelines. Rogers not only handled Roepke's punts faultlessly but also made the longest run of the afternoon when he circled left end for 22 yards in the final period.

Penn's lighter line outplayed Bezdek's line, but the secondary defense of Penn State tightened whenever Penn advanced the ball beyond midfield.

Cy Lungreen, a Philadelphia boy, playing quarterback for Penn State, did not use very good judgment in running the plays and finally gave way to John Pincura, who was an improvement both in running the ball and diagnosing Penn's defense.

Coach Lou Young's Penn team stuck to a straight running attack most of the time, trying 10 passes but only two worked for a total of 33 yards. In first downs, Penn had 11 to State's five.

Penn's "hidden ball" functioned spasmodically. Whenever it looked as though the Red and Blue ballcarriers were headed for a touchdown, something always happened to slow them up.

Paul Murphy's punting gave Penn an advantage in the first half. This helped in the march that took the ball into Penn State territory and gave Scull a chance to try for a field goal. He grasped the ball like a veteran. On the first play of the second period, Scull again tried a drop kick from the 35-yard line, but it went a few yards to the right of the goal posts.

In rushing and forward passes, Penn gained 213 yards to State's 145. State tried 13 forward passes, six being successful for a gain of 78 yards. Penn tried 10 passes but only two worked for 33 yards.

Penn State 10 Pittsburgh 0

November 25, 1939 | State College, Pa.

Penn State Tops Pitt, 10-0; First Win Over Panthers Since 1919

By Claire M. Burcky

The Pittsburgh Press

Pittsburgh	0	0	0	0 —	0
Penn	7	0	0	3 —	10

By the score of 10-0, a touchdown, an extra point, and a field goal, Penn State defeated Pitt here today, to record the first Lion triumph over the Panthers since 1919, when young Bob Higgins, now Coach Bob Higgins, captained a Nittany outfit that tied a 20-0 knot into the tail of the Panther.

And virtually every man, woman and child in the overflow crowd of 20,000 fans was ready tonight to celebrate, to tear the town wide open over an occurrence that when it comes no more often than once every 20 years, must be observed fittingly, even fightingly.

There were a few fights, flaring suddenly and ending just as abruptly, as students struggled to tear down the goal posts, but once they had uprooted them, they marched away happily, arm in arm, to make the most of the occasion.

"We realized we had a chance to win, and we were up for the game," Higgins said between handshakes with old grads in the Lion dressing room after the battle.

Penn State was ready, no question of that. The Lions dominated Pitt as no team has dominated the Panthers all season. They rolled up a net gain of 165 yards in 17 first downs, threatened to score one or more times in every quarter, and kept the Panthers most of the afternoon from getting away from the Pitt side of the field.

State unloosed two powerful fullbacks in Lloyd Ickes and Bill Smaltz, a pair of swift halfbacks in Chuck Peters and John Petrella, and a savage line that revolved around Leon Gajecki, the center, who waded through the game's entire 60 minutes to be singled out by Higgins as the one player deserving greatest praise in the victory.

Pitt's rushing gains totaled 166 yards but the alert Gajecki, abetted by

Bob Higgins was 91-57-11 as Penn State's head football coach from 1930-1948.

a pair of smashing ends, Tom Vargo and Spike Alter of Pittsburgh, never let the Panthers threaten seriously. The Penn State line smeared Pitt plays for more than 60 yards, held the Panthers passing to two completions for 16 yards, and blocked with the devastation of a tidal wave as Peters ran up and down the field for 10, 15 and sometimes 20 yards at a clip.

The Panthers played in spurts, at times shooting their ballcarriers forward for sizeable gains that appeared certain to reach the goal line. Too often, however, overeagerness in the line produced offsides that frequently provided too much of a handicap to overcome.

As a matter of fact, there were 19 penalties in the game, eight against Penn State and 11 against Pitt. Eighty-five yards were measured off against the Panthers, and this, with five fumbles, counted heavily in the final reckoning.

The Lions threatened twice in the early minutes before they finally sent Smaltz across from the 1-yard line with the opening score, moments before the first quarter ended.

A couple of passes by Smaltz, one by Craig White for 22 yards and another to Peters for 13, gave Penn State their first chance, and when Peters came out of a fake placekick to run for a first down, the Lions were going strong and on Pitt's 23-yard line.

But Pitt wasn't ready to yield a score yet. Jack Goodridge gave the Panthers the lift they needed by spilling Smaltz for a 13-yard loss on a pass attempt, and the Panthers got out of that by taking the ball at their 38.

In the next 10 seconds, Pitt came closest to a score. Dandy Dick Cassiano, with Ben Kish serving as acting captain, followed a wave of the best blocking he has been given in many games, got into the clear around left end with one blocker still leading him, and raced 33 yards downfield. Cassiano started his run down the west sideline, but at the

Leon Gajecki, an all-America center in 1940.

Penn State 35, he swerved toward midfield to let another blocker get ahead of him, and then was caught from behind at the Lions 29.

Immediately, the overeager Panthers were handed two offside penalties and Gajecki spilled Bob Thurbon for a 5-yard loss on a reverse. Smaltz stopped the threat completely by intercepting Cassiano's pass to Thurbon and carting it back some 30 yards to the Pitt 40, where Ted Konetsky came up in the nick of time to crash him out of bounds.

This started the Lions goalward again, but Joe Connell averted a score by deflecting a Smaltz to White touchdown pass, and John Patrick's field goal attempt from the Pitt 37 was wide.

But the fates ruled that Penn State should have her score. It came in just three plays, after Cassiano fumbled and Gajecki tumbled on the ball on the Pitt 22. Peters slashed outside left tackle for 3 yards, and White took a reverse from Smaltz to the 1–yard line, where Cassiano flung him out of bounds. But the delay was only a moment, for Smaltz punched it over on the next play and Ben Pollock, a reserve tackle who had missed only three extra-point tries in two seasons, booted across the seventh point.

The Lions were back on their side of the field early in the second quarter when two roughing penalties against Pitt, one for unnecessary roughness and another for running into the kicker, gave them first down on the Panther 36.

Ickes heaved a pass good for 13 yards to Gil Radcliff, and then the Lion fullback took a spinner through the middle for first down on the Pitt 13. But Pitt rode out this threat when Mike Sekela chased Petrella back on a reverse, nearly yanked his head off with a one-handed tackle, and caused Petrella to fumble. Art Corace recovered the ball on the Pitt 21. And they sparred, gingerly, for the rest of the half.

There were long runs in the third quarter, but no serious threats. Emil Narick broke away for one of 19 yards, and White equalled it for State. George Kracum clicked off a 15-yard end run, and Narick got another for 15, but the Panthers had started from their own 11 and got only to midfield when the quarter ended.

Forced back to their own 5-yard line by Ickes' punt and an ensuing offside penalty, Kish, playing with a leg fracture in a heavy cast from ankle to knee, contributed a kick that was the punting highlight of the game. Standing deep in his end zone, he sent a low kick that traveled midfield to the State 46.

Penn State appeared to be halted by an offside penalty when Peters suddenly shook free around right end for 22 yards on a march that wound up in the final score. Ickes took over and spun down the middle for another 10. Peters bowled along for another 5, before Hal Klein and Harry Kindelberger smeared a couple of plays. And then, on fourth down with 3 yards to go, John Patrick toed a field goal squarely between the uprights from the 24, for the feat that erased virtually all Pitt hope for a tie.

Pitt hung on gamely, but futilely, for the last five minutes. Narick knocked off a 15-yard run, and Edgar Jones tossed a pass to Kish that gained 14 yards and first down on the Penn State 25.

But Vargo tossed in a monkey wrench by spilling Jones for a 13-yard loss on a pass attempt, a fumble in the backfield dropped four more, and the alert Penn State secondary thwarted aerial attempts.

Penn State 13 SMU 13

January 1, 1948 | Dallas, Tex.

Chilly Cotton Bowl Ends in Tie Between Penn State, SMU

By Chester L. Smith

The Pittsburgh Press

| Penn State | 0 | 7 | 6 | 0 | — | 13 |
| Southern Methodist | 7 | 6 | 0 | 0 | — | 13 |

The man who makes the Cotton Bowl trophies went back to work today with a rush order on his hands. He had to hammer out an extra copy. One will go to Penn State and the other to Southern Methodist to symbolize the 13-13 tie they played here before some 47,000 assorted and well-refrigerated Texans and Pennsylvanians, who carried virtually every hotel blanket in town to the stadium to fend off the chilly wind that whistled down from the north.

Most tie games leave a bad taste and provide a field day for the volunteer quarterbacks, but this one didn't. As the teams played it out, there was complete justice done all around. Anything else would have been entirely out of order.

Each side scored a couple of well-earned touchdowns and each bobbled one of the conversions. Larry Cooney, the reserve halfback from Langley High School of Pittsburgh, and Wally Triplett, the right half from Philadelphia, had touchdowns for the Lions. Paul Page and Doak Walker tallied for the Mustangs.

Walker was true with his first conversion, but wild on the second. The same thing happened to Ed Czekaj, Penn State's point-after-touchdown specialist.

Elwood Petchel, the tiny tyke from Easton, pitched both of Penn State's scores. To justify his glittering advance notices, Walker threw the first one for Southern Methodist and jammed over from the 2 for the second.

This was hardly a game that will be written into football primers for future generations to copy. It was played fiercely, but the good blocking and tackling was interspersed with some that was extremely mediocre. There were fumbles that hurt both sides, plus intercepted passes and

34

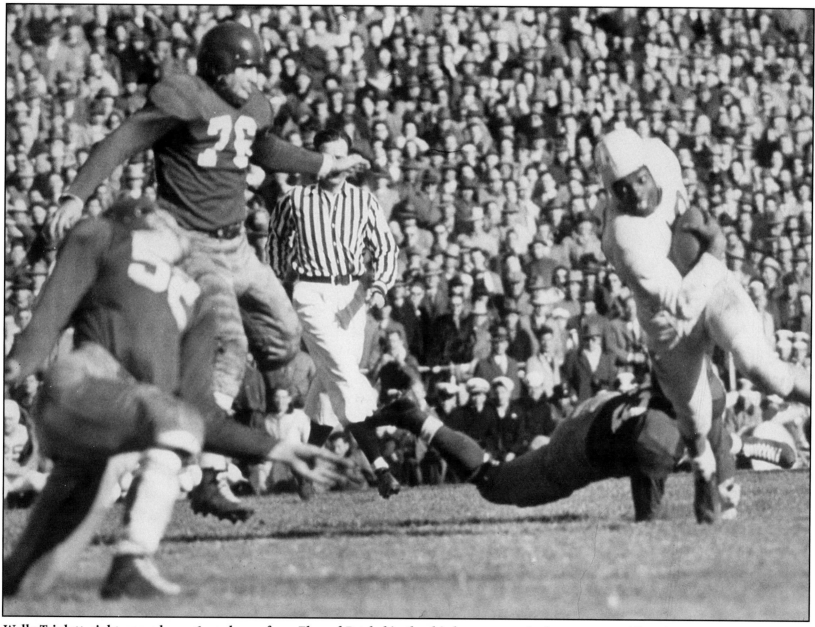

Wally Triplett, right, scored on a 6-yard pass from Elwood Petchel in the third quarter to tie the score at 13. The Nittany Lions' extra-point attempt, though, was no good, again. Neither team could score in the fourth quarter.

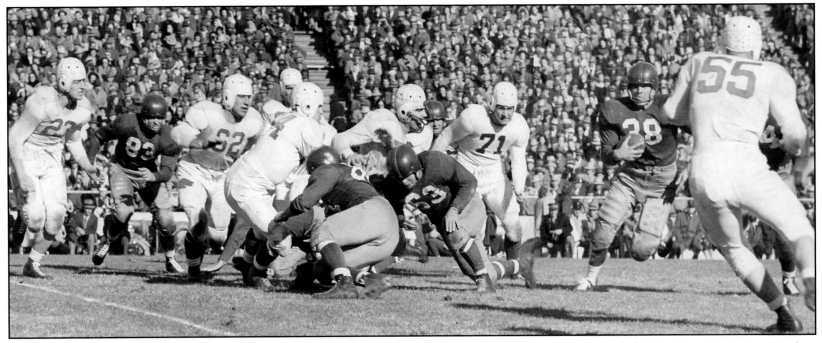

Penn State's John Wolosky (55) and Neg Norton (71) close in on Southern Methodist's Dick McKissick (38) during the 1948 Cotton Bowl.

mishandling of the ball, especially in the Ponies backfield.

Even the two all-Americans finished in a dead heat for honors. Walker enjoyed a tremendous first half, while Penn State's Steve Suhey was finding the going most embarrassing. Then, in the last two periods, Suhey found himself and Walker almost dropped out of the picture.

The deadlock allowed both teams to write their seasons into the records as the year of no defeats. For Southern Methodist it was their second tie (19-19 with TCU in the regular schedule's finale) and for Penn State it was the first time the Lions have walked off the field without being victors since the Pitt game of 1946.

The Ponies had their 13 points before the Easterners could break through. The Lions were the aggressors at first. Taking the ball on their 48 after Walker had kicked short off the side of his foot, they plowed

ahead to the 17, where Earl Cook, the SMU guard, barreled Bobby Williams inches short of a first down, allowing the Mustangs to take over. Francis Rogel, the sophomore fullback from North Braddock and as good a ball carrier as there was on the field, did most of the bucking and slanting in this march.

But the Ponies kicked back hard. Walker ran and passed them close to their 47, then faded from his tailback position and threw high and far to Page. The latter outran Jeff Durkota, took the ball over his shoulder near the sideline and had no opposition as he sprinted goalward.

The Lions had little poise for the remainder of the first quarter.

Early in the second quarter they forced the Ponies to punt from their 36, only to lose the advantage by being offside. It was a first down, instead, and Southern Methodist hustled all the way to Penn State's 30 before Cooney batted down a fourth-down pass to allow the Lions to take over.

For the next 10 minutes the Blue and White had more trouble than they could handle. Gil Johnson passed the Mustangs to the 8-yard line, where Cooney recovered a fumble by Dick McKissack. The Southwest Conference champions were back a moment later when Johnson began pitching once more.

It was McKissack, however, who put the stranglehold on Penn State. He slipped through their left guard from the 21 to the 2, leaving Walker with nothing more than a light jab at the middle for the touchdown.

It looked then like the Mustangs' game, but in the last minutes of the half Petchel pulled the Lions back into contention.

Petchel opened with a 13-yard pass to Bob Hicks from the Lions' 35, then ran for 20 yards after faking a throw. Triplett was thrown for a loss, and only seconds remained. But after he had twice missed his target, Petchel found Cooney in the end zone and connected. Czekaj converted and the Lions were roaring for the first time.

They took complete charge of the ceremonies in the second half.

SMU had the ball scarcely three minutes in the third period. The Mustangs held on the 1-foot line after a 42-yard advance, but their fine work was rubbed out when Petchel brought Ed Green's punt back to the 9. Two bucks by Rogel put the ball on the 4, and Petchel connected with Triplett in the end zone on third down.

State got as far as the Ponies' 30 in the last quarter and Southern Methodist was once the same distance from the Lions' goal line.

Intercepted passes and a deal of exemplary defending by the Lion secondaries were the vital factors in preventing any scores in the fourth quarter.

The finish was hair-raising. With time for only one play, Petchell dodged four Mustang rushers and hurled the ball 45 yards into the end zone. It was aimed for Dennie Hoggard, the end. He was there, but the throw was at his knees. It trickled off his hands as the gun sounded.

Steve Suhey, an all-America guard in 1947.

THE RIP ENGLE ERA

What no one had figured was that halfback Lenny Moore would suddenly throw off the cloak of despair and return to his hero pedestal. The second leading ground gainer in the nation last year, the Lions great hasn't even been in the Top 20 this campaign.
But he came up with an old-time performance just when it was needed most. In Coach Rip Engle's jubilant words, "Lenny never in his life was greater."

Carl Hugher
The Pittsburgh Press

Penn State 14 Illinois 12

September 25, 1954 | Champaign, Ill.

THE RIP ENGLE ERA

'Reading Rambler' Leads Lions Past Big Ten Champions

By Chester L. Smith

The Pittsburgh Press

Penn State	7	7	0	0 —	14
Illinois	6	0	6	0 —	12

Penn State threw a numbing shock into the largest crowd that has seen an opening game in Memorial Stadium here this afternoon by turning back Illinois, the defending co-champions of the Big Ten, 14-12. The 54,094 who sat in heat that was better suited to a dip in a cool pond than football saw more than an upset; they got an eyeful of a back who proved himself fully the equal of the Illini's magician, J.C. Caroline. This young gentleman was Lenny Moore, the "Reading Rambler," who was in the Orange and Blue's hair all afternoon.

The teams matched touchdowns — a pair apiece — but Penn State co-captain Jim Garrity of Monaca proved the difference when he kicked both extra points, while Caroline and Bob Wiman were wide and low on both their attempts to tack on the seventh point.

Jesse Arnelle and Moore were Penn State's scorers. The former gathered in a 24-yard pass from Pittsburgh's Don Bailey — who was a highly competent quarterback today — in the end zone late in the opening period. Bailey also was the key man in the second touchdown when, shortly before the intermission, he sped to his left on Illinois' 18 and lateraled to Moore, who zigged and zagged past three would-be tacklers to cross the goal line not more than a yard from the sideline.

Abe Woodson, Caroline's sophomore running mate, scored twice for the Illini. He gave his side a 6-0 lead before the game was five minutes old by taking a short screen pass from Em Lindbeck, thrown from the State 28, and out-tricking the defense to go the remaining 26 yards.

His second touchdown in the third quarter was a 17-yard cutback through State's right side.

There was magnificent work today on both sides. Rosy Grier, the Lions' mammoth left tackle, wrapped himself around Illini ballcarriers

Lenny Moore, the Reading Rambler, scored the game-winning touchdown to defeat Illinois.

time after time, while his sidekick, Arnelle, smothered at least a half-dozen plays that kept Penn State in the game. Jan Smid, the Illinois captain, was responsible more than anyone else for preventing the Lions from running wild. His performance today stamped him as one of the country's great guards.

But it was the Caroline-Moore duel that intrigued the onlookers. Caroline gained 115 yards for an average of 6.4 per try, but Moore came away with the edge — 124 yards and an average of 7.3

An intercepted pass and a penalty that appeared harmless when it was stepped off gave Illinois its scoring opportunities.

Lindbeck picked off a throw by Bailey shortly after the kickoff on his 35 and scurried to State's 42. Caroline and Mickey Bates rushed for a first down on the 31. Woodson added three yards and then took Lindbeck's pitch to put the Illini ahead, 12-7.

Penn State took the lead before the period ended. Moore had returned a punt to Illinois' 37 and the Lions had worked their way to the 32 when they were stopped by a second interception. But Bates promptly fumbled the ball into Arnelle's hands on the 28, and three plays later Arnelle was behind the goal line with Bailey's toss in his arms.

Penn State lineman Rosy Grier.

41

Penn State 21 Syracuse 20

November 5, 1955 | State College, Pa.

Moore Outshines Syracuse's Brown in Lions' Victory

By Carl Hughes

The Pittsburgh Press

There's no law against Syracuse winning a football game at Penn State, but there might as well be. The frustrated Orange hasn't won here in 21 years, but it appeared for most of this afternoon that this time things would be different.

Bet when the points were totaled at the end, it was the same old story — although closer than usual: Penn State 21, Syracuse 20.

Certainly even the most rabid Nittany Lions fans in the sellout throng of 30,321 — let alone the Orange rooters — doubted early in the third quarter that State had a chance.

What no one had figured was that halfback Lenny Moore would suddenly throw off the cloak of despair and return to his hero pedestal. The second leading ground gainer in the nation last year, the Lions great hasn't even been in the Top 20 this campaign.

But he came up with an old-time performance just when it was needed most. In Coach Rip Engle's jubilant words, "Lenny never in his life

Syracuse	7	6	7	0 —	20
Penn State	0	7	7	7 —	21

was greater."

The senior from Reading put Penn State back in the game almost on his own and then took it away from the stunned Orange. He gained 146 yards on 22 carries — by far his biggest day of the season.

Oddly enough, he was outgained by another terrific halfback — Syracuse's Jim Brown. The Orange ace had 155 yards on 20 carries, scored all his team's touchdowns and two extra points, and threatened to turn the contest into a runaway for the New Yorkers.

Moore wasn't Penn State's only hero, of course. Quarterback Milt Plum not only kicked the three vital extra points, but played 50 minutes — about twice as much as any other signal caller for the Lions this season.

On one play, however, the biggest hero of all was Jack Farls, a substitute sophomore end from Freedom. He broke through to block one of Brown's extra-point tries to provide what eventually was the winning margin.

It didn't seem too important at the time, though. It still left Syracuse ahead, 13-0, midway in the second quarter, and the Orange seemed to be unstoppable.

Their first score came the second time they got the ball, after a Plum fumble was nabbed at the State 29. Brown stormed to the 8 on the first carry and, four plays later, he dove to a touchdown from the 2.

The second Syracuse tally was not earned as easily. It came at the end of a 68–yard drive the next time the Orange had possession.

The Lions thought momentarily that they had halted the march, but a fourth-down pass from the 6 thrown by quarterback Ed Albright was snagged by the inevitable Brown on the goal line.

Penn State, meanwhile, was making no threatening gestures and it wasn't until the half almost had run out that the Lions scored. There was just a minute to play when Albright strangely passed from his own 33.

Fullback Joe Sabol intercepted the ill-timed toss and shook off some four or five tacklers as he returned 28 yards down the sideline to the 10. Plum flipped the ball to Billy Kane on the first play and the Munhall halfback stepped the last 2 yards into the end zone.

That left the Orange anything but discouraged. They roared back to a two-touchdown lead in just seven plays at the start of the second half.

Brown returned the kickoff 47 yards to put the march in motion. He finally burst through from the 6 to score. His extra point gave Syracuse a 20–7 lead but proved to be the visitors' last tally of the afternoon.

After that, Moore came to life and lifted the whole Penn State team up with him. The Lions moved to a touchdown following the kickoff, with a Plum pass to Kane for 19 yards, the biggest gainer. Moore took care of most of the carrying chores and finally exploded across from the 2.

Syracuse threatened to increase its margin back to two touchdowns

Dan Radakovich (51) receives instruction from Penn State coach Rip Engle, left, and assistant Frank Patrick.

at the start of of the final quarter. A Plum pass had been intercepted by Brown and moments later the Syracuse halfback ripped 42 yards to the State 13. But Plum got revenge and also nipped the threat when he snagged an Albright toss in the end zone.

The Lions were given the ball on their 20, of course, and they smashed 30 yards to the winning touchdown, with Moore and fullback Bill Straub of Allison Park doing much of the smashing. The score, though, came on a 1–yard sneak by Plum.

Then he stepped back and converted the winning point.

A Syracuse fumble three plays after the kickoff was claimed by guard Sam Valentine for State at the Orange 46. That not only checked the visitors, but the Lions roared to the enemy 2 before time ran out.

Penn State 7 Ohio State 6

October 20, 1956 | Columbus, Ohio

THE RIP ENGLE ERA

Nittany Lions Dash Ohio State's Hopes for National Title

By Bob Drum

The Pittsburgh Press

Penn State	0	0	0	7 —	7
Ohio State	0	0	0	0 —	6

The Penn State Lions came into this football-mad town cubs but left full-grown maneaters. And when they left, the Lions took with them Ohio State's hopes for a national championship. While 82,584 fans sat on their hands waiting for a chance to cheer, the Penn State line manhandled its bigger opponent, and quarterback Milt Plum guided the offense to a 7-6 victory.

It was Penn State from start to finish except for two brief spurts by the Buckeyes that ran nearly the length of the field. The Bucks, seeking their ninth-straight victory and fourth of the season, were favored by as many as three touchdowns before the game.

Columbus fans figured it to be an easy Saturday for their favorites prior to five straight Big Ten contests in defense of the championship the Bucks have won two years running. But they were wrong.

The Lions outrushed a team that had been averaging 333 yards on the ground and made them change their mode of attack. In three pre-vious games, Ohio State had thrown only 41 passes, but had run over the opposition with a relentless ground attack.

Today, the Buckeyes had to take to the air to get their only score and throw 10 passes in a desperate attempt to confuse the Lion line.

It was Plum who kicked the conversion that eventually was the difference. It was also Plum, a senior quarterback, who turned a mistake into the game-saving play. With third down and a yard to go for a touchdown, Plum juggled the ball and missed a handoff to sophomore Bruce Gilmore. Plum never lost poise, though.

He looked around and set sail through the middle of the Ohio State line to the 24-yard line and a first down.

A moment later, it was Plum who took charge again. With third down and 8 yards to go — and the Penn State bench pleading for him to get in position for a fourth-down field goal — Plum elected to pass.

He spotted Munhall's Billy Kane open on the 5-yard line and hit him right in the midsection with a pass. Kane carried right to the goal line and needed only a foot to make a score.

The quick-thinking quarterback tried two sneaks and then elected to let Gilmore go for the score with only 3:35 left to play. It was a fitting reward, for it was Gilmore who got two first downs in the key series which carried to the score.

A fantastic punt by Plum set up the winning drive early in the fourth quarter. He kicked the ball while standing behind his 20-yard line. The punt carried over the safety man's head and rolled out of bounds on the Ohio 3.

The Lions' touchdown seemed to instill new life into Ohio State. Following Plum's kickoff, the Buckeyes began to roll.

Sophomore Don Clark rushed for a first down to the 32, but the Bucks decided there wasn't enough time left to grind out the winning score, so they took to the air.

Jimmy Roseboro passed to end Leo Brown for a first down on the Penn State 40. On the next play, Brown got down the right sideline unnoticed by Penn State halfback Ray Alberigi.

Roseboro tossed to him at the 15 and Brown was pushed out of bounds on a desperate lunge by Alberigi at the 4. But it was to no avail since Clark ran over right guard for a touchdown on the next play with 1:58 left to play.

Sophomore Frank Kremblas, who had missed a field goal earlier in the game from the 25, was sent in for the placement. Coach Woody Hayes of Ohio State also sent in another substitution just before Kremblas tried his kick and the Buckeyes were penalized for 12 men on the field.

Next, Kremblas had to kick from the 14. It was a long kick that went wide to the left as Penn State's bench went whooping with joy.

It was the largest crowd to watch a Penn State showing.

Milt Plum, who later starred for the Cleveland Browns and Detroit Lions in the NFL, completed 40 of 75 passes for 675 yards and six touchdowns in 1956.

Penn State 7 Alabama 0

December 19, 1959 | Philadelphia, Pa.

THE RIP ENGLE ERA

Scrappy Lions Defeat Alabama in Liberty Bowl

By Roy McHugh

The Pittsburgh Press

Penn State	0	7	0	0 —	7
Alabama	0	0	0	0 —	0

Penn State's football team allowed precious few liberties to Alabama today in the Liberty Bowl. The Nittany Lions were unable to take many themselves, but they conned their way to finesse a touchdown as time ran out in the first half and it stood up the rest of the day for a 7-0 victory. There were five seconds to play in the first half when Penn State hopped into a field-goal formation on the Crimson Tide's 18-yard line.

Instead of holding the ball for Sam Stellatella's placekick, however, sophomore quarterback Galen Hall threw a screen pass to sophomore halfback Roger Kochman of Wilkinsburg out on the left flank.

Alabama fell for the carpetbag trick hook, line and sinker. With an escort of four blockers, Kochman stormed down the sideline, weaving in and out as he went.

There was a shattering open-field block by Tom Mulraney and when Kochman got to the 3-yard line, where someone at last had a shot at him, he merely launched himself into the air and came down in the end zone head first. By that time the clock had run out.

Stellatella kicked the extra point and, thereafter, nothing much happened.

The 36, 211 spectators had to turn up their coat collars against a 20-mph wind from the north, but otherwise it was not a bad day for football — benevolent as anyone could hope for on this side of the Mason-Dixon line in December.

The bright blue sky would have done credit to New Orleans or Houston or Dallas and there were no reports of anyone freezing to death.

For Alabama, the wind was an ill wind. It blew no good to the Crimson Tide just before Kochman's touchdown, taking a high punt by

46

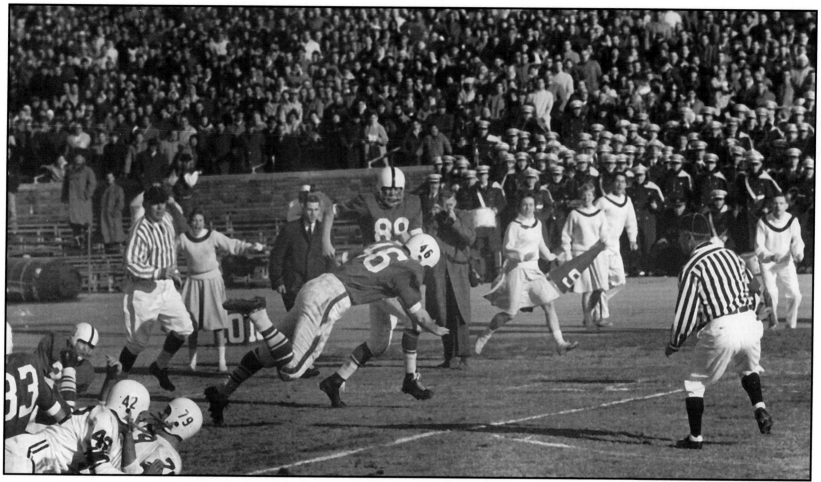

Penn State's Roger Kochman (46) lunges into the end zone for the only touchdown of the 1959 Liberty Bowl against Alabama. Kochman scored on a pass from quarterback Galen Hall after a fake field goal late in the first half.

fullback Tommy White back toward the line of scrimmage. When the ball came to rest, it had traveled four yards horizontally.

But there were 22 yards between State and the goal line and the Lions had to get there in 30 seconds. Furthermore, they had to get there without Richie Lucas.

Felled by a hip injury — a bruise that practically immobilized him

— Lucas had left the game after playing just a little over a quarter. In that short time he had gained more ground than anyone else was to gain all day — 54 yards running and 23 passing.

When Hall took his place, it was Penn State's ball on the Alabama 28-yard line, where Jay Huffman had recovered a fumble. Hall took the Lions inside to the 5, making two first downs himself, but there

THE
RIP ENGL
ERA

47

Before the 1959 Liberty Bowl, three Penn State quarterbacks — from left, Rich Lucas, Galen Hall and Bob Ghigiarelli — knew they faced a difficult task. The 52 on the chalkboard is the total number of points Alabama allowed in the regular season.

Alabama held for three plays.

On fourth down from the 1, Hall threw a rollout pass into the end zone. Alabama's corner linebacker butted it high in the air, giving Bob Mitinger a chance to make the catch. But Mitinger dropped the ball.

It was only a reprieve for Alabama. Gary O'Steen punted into the wind and Penn State had the ball again on the Alabama 19.

The Lions got to the 5 and Stellatella actually did try a field goal, but

Billy Richardson blocked it. There was 2:30 left in the half.

Alabama ran three plays and then had to punt again. White needn't have bothered. The wind-blown kick went from the 18-yard line to the 22.

Hall threw a screen pass to Pat Botula, gaining four yards and then came the play that won the ball game.

Alabama came here billed as the toughest defensive team in the

Poor weather forced the Nittany Lions to hold some very cold practice sessions. From left, Galen Hall, Tom Mulraney and Dick Hoak pose on a particularly cold afternoon with snowballs, rather than footballs.

Southeastern Conference, and though Penn State wound up with 278 yards on the ground, the Lions hammered it out bit by bit.

There were two long drives. Lucas started one by tearing 24 yards on a keeper play after O'Steen's quick-kick with the wind at his back rolled out of bounds on the 3 — 61 yards from the line of scrimmage.

Throwing one pass — for 23 yards to John Bozick — Lucas moved Penn State to the Alabama 9, where Kochman fumbled. This was in the opening period, and the Lions never really controlled the ball again until the fourth period.

They used up the last seven minutes going from their own 38 to the Alabama 10, every inch of the way on the ground. Satisfied with a seven-point win, they let the last 20 seconds tick off without even trying to run another play.

Penn State had one other scoring chance when Frank Korbini recovered a fumble on Alabama's 27-yard line early in the game. Nothing came of it.

Alabama got the ball on a fumble in Penn State territory once, but fumbled right back. The exchange ended up on the Penn State 28 and that was high tide for Alabama.

The Crimson Tide's longest drive was 35 yards to the Penn State 38, where the Lions held for downs.

"Hard line play was what won it for us," Coach Rip Engle said. "We beat them at their own game."

Bearing out Engle's opinion, Chuck Janerrette was equally outstanding.

Engle, by the way, sent in the play that scored the touchdown. The Lions had never tried it before and practiced it only twice all season.

Bob Mitinger, an
all-America end in 1961.

THE RIP ENGLE ERA

Penn State 41 Oregon 12

December 17, 1960 | Philadelphia, Pa.

Hoak Shoots Down Ducks in Liberty Bowl Thriller

United Press International

The Pittsburgh Press

Dick Hoak, a No. 2 quarterback of a No. 1 magnitude, picked up a trailing Penn State team today and led two units of the Nittany Lions to a 41-12 rout of Oregon in the ice-fringed second annual Liberty Bowl game.

Penn State	0	21	0	20	41
Oregon	6	0	6	0	12

Hoak, the boss-man of the Lions' second unit, dubbed the "Ready Team" by Coach Rip Engle, hit the Oregon trail after the Webfoots scored a first-period touchdown, and by overcoming goal line adversity, led Penn State to three touchdowns in the second period to put the game in the deep freeze.

The 185-pound senior from Jeannette, Pa., not only had a hand in five of the Lions' six touchdowns, but scored two himself — one on a six-yard dash with a ballet leap into the end zone in the second period and his second on a 11-yard rollout in the fourth.

His brilliant fourth period performance saw him crowd his 11-yard touchdown sprint, an interception and a 33-yard touchdown pass to halfback Dick Pae, all in the space of four minutes.

Hoak, who won the game's Most Valuable Player Award warmed up 16,624 spectators scattered like pepper dust in the 97,000-seat Philadelphia Stadium with standout performances in all departments.

He probed the Webfoots' line with searching astuteness, ran when he had to, and passed with objectiveness which kept the one-touchdown underdog Oregon off balance.

The Webfoots, who unfortunately lost halfback Cleveland Jones on the first play from scrimmage with a kidney injury after he caught a 12-yard pass, broke into the scoring column with a first period 88-yard drive in 12 plays with quarterback Dave Grosz going over from the 1.

Then, Hoak and his No. 2 unit, which yielded the Ducks' score, took

50

The 1960 offensive attack which defeated Oregon: Jim Kerr (41) carrying the ball with Dick Hoak (23), Bill Popp (64), Al Jacks (24) and Sam Sobczak (45) blocking.

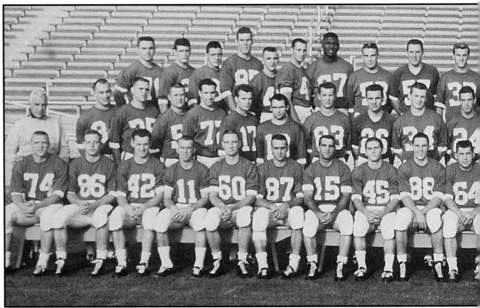

Roger Kochman, an all-America halfback in 1962.

command. The Lions began a march on their 37, gambled successfully twice on fourth down running plays, and drew one break when a missed pass found a substitution delay by Oregon keeping the drive alive.

Hoak made the most of the break as the second period opened to send State to a first down on the Oregon 12 and threw a pass to Henry Oppermann, who was borrowed from the first unit, for a first down on the Oregon 1. Don Jonas, also on lend-lease from the first unit, went over from the 1 and when Oppermann, voted the most valuable lineman, converted Penn State had a 7-6 lead it never lost.

Then a 1-yard adversity struck. Penn State's first unit moved from its 20 following a punt and went as far as the Oregon 1. But Sam Sobczak fumbled into the end zone and Oregon recovered.

Jonas returned the ensuing punt 23 yards to the Oregon 37, and Hoak ran for 12 yards to the 26. Hoak followed with an 11-yard run to the 1. Penn State was offside on the next play but three 2-yard bolts sent Al Gursky over and Penn State led, 14-6.

The Lions' posted a 7-3 -0 record in 1960.

Hoak personally took charge of the next score when he swept six yards into the end zone with 31 seconds left in the half to make it 21-6.

The Webfoots scored in the third period with Dave Grayson — voted the game's outstanding back — running 10 yards over guard.

Then the Lions, with the No. 1 unit in action, opened the fourth period chopping their way from their own five and in 15 plays Ed Caye went over from the one.

Hoak scored the next TD on his 11-yard run.

Hoak called it a day with an interception and a 15-yard return to Oregon's 33. The Lions quarterback then floated Pae into the open and hit him with a pass for the final touchdown of the game.

It was the Lions' second straight Liberty Bowl victory. They beat Alabama 7-0 in the first Liberty Bowl game last year.

Rip Engle and his 1960 team captain Hank Oppermann.

Penn State receiver Jack Curry (81) jumps high for a pass in the end zone against Georgia Tech defender Mike Page. Lions quarterback Galen Hall threw three scoring passes against Tech, leading Penn State to a 30-15 victory.

Penn State 30 Georgia Tech 15

December 30, 1961 | Jacksonville, Fla.

Hall's TD Passes Lead Lions to Gator Bowl Victory

By Chester L. Smith

The Pittsburgh Press

Quarterback Galen Hall threw three touchdown passes leading Penn State to a 30-15 victory over Georgia Tech today before 50,202 fans in the Gator Bowl.

After Penn State trailed, 9-0, in the second quarter, Hall fired a pair of TD passes for a 14-9 halftime edge and added another to put the Lions in front, 20-9, after three quarters.

Tech scored a last-quarter touchdown, but State came back with a field goal by Don Jonas and another touchdown.

Georgia Tech won the toss and chose to receive.

Jonas' kickoff went to the Tech 24. Jake Martin took it and ran to the Tech 37. Stanley Gann went wide to the left for 11 yards.

Two more running plays earned Tech a first down at the Penn State 40, but three additional rushes netted only seven yards and Tech's Billy Lotheridge punted out of bounds at the Penn State 10.

After an offsides penalty, Roger Kochman rushed to the 9. On second down, Hall threw wild to the sidelines. Officials ruled he grounded the

Penn State	0	14	6	10 —	30
Georgia Tech	2	7	0	6 —	15

ball intentionally and granted Tech a safety.

On the free kick from its 20, Penn State's Pete Liske punted to William Williamson at the Tech 30 and he returned to the Tech 49. After a first down at the State 36, Tech lost two yards in three attempts and Lotheridge's punt was over the goal line.

On second down, Kochman moved to the 36 for 12 yards and a first down, but Tech had Penn State in trouble again when Hall fumbled and Frank Sexton recovered at the 33.

A Gann pass was intercepted by Pete Liske in the end zone.

Forced to punt without a first down, Penn State was again in trouble after a Lotheridge to Williamson pass covered 44 yards to a first down on the Penn State 8.

55

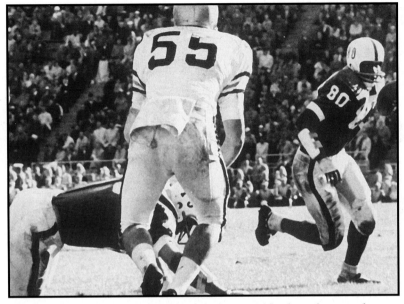

Penn State's Dave Robinson (80) picks up a block and turns the corner against Georgia Tech's Bobby Caldwell. Robinson had four receptions in the 1961 Gator Bowl.

Dave Robinson, an all-America end in 1962.

On second down, Bill Saul recovered Lotheridge's fumble at the 8 as the quarter ended.

Tech started a touchdown drive after a punt rolled dead on the Tech 20. Williamson got five yards and Joseph Auer picked up seven to the 32. Then Auer dashed 68 yards to the end zone. The conversion was good.

Harold Powell returned the kickoff 17 yards to the Penn State 22. Two running plays netted seven yards, then Hall passed to Kochman for nine yards and a first down at the Penn State 38 and to Dave Robinson, who caught it on the dead run up the middle for 21 yards to the Tech 38. Buddy Torris picked up 3 yards, then Hall tossed to Dick Anderson on the right sidelines for 14 yards to the 21. Al Gursky drove for eight to the 13.

Hall fired toward Gursky, who dove desperately for the ball and gathered it inches from the near-frozen ground in the end zone. Jonas converted.

With only three minutes remaining Penn State's Kochman rushed for 14 yards to the Lions' 27. Hall connected with Anderson for nine yards and out of bounds stopping the clock with the ball at the Lions' 36.

James Powell carried for 13 yards to the Penn State 49, then came an offside penalty against the Lions. But Hall hit Robinson on the sidelines for 10 yards and Anderson down the middle for 16 yards to the Tech 30. State called time out and there were only one minute 12 seconds remaining.

A screen pass from Hall to Anderson was good for three yards. Hall faded and looped one to Kochman for a coffin-corner catch and Penn State's second touchdown.

This was the first time in 1961 that Georgia Tech's defense had surrendered two touchdowns in a game. Jonas converted.

Penn State punted to Tech's 22. A Gann keeper got a first down at the 38, but Joe Blasentine recovered a Tech fumble at the Georgia 46. Nothing worthwhile materialized for the Lions and Liske punted over the goal.

Three Tech plays gained five yards, then Lotheridge punted to the Penn State 29. Rushing three times, the Lions were inches short of a first down and Liske punted to the Tech 18.

Gann moved Tech to two first downs on the ground to the Tech 43. On second down, Dave Robinson boomed through the Engineer line and not only smeared a fading Gann, but stole the ball at the Tech 35.

On the first play, that quick lineup Penn State used against Pitt and Syracuse worked again. Hall pitched to Powell, all alone down the right side and Penn State had a third touchdown. The conversion was fouled up by an offside line.

Fourth Quarter

Thanks to a Lotheridge to Williamson pass play of 12 yards, Tech had a first down at the Penn State 35. But an errant pass and two futile runs netted a lost yard and conservative Tech elected to punt from the 36, the ball sailing out of the end zone.

Lacking a first down, Liske punted — the ball sailing low into the hands of Toner at midfield. He got four yards on the return, was gang-tackled and Penn State came out of it losing 15 yards on a penalty to its own 36.

On next play, a Lotheridge pitchout was wild, but Auer hustled back and scooped it up at the 25, then danced and skipped down the side for Tech's second TD. Gann's two-point running try was short.

With less than five minutes left, Penn State took the ball at the Tech 12 when the Engineers gambled on fourth down with a fake-punt screen pass, which fell incomplete.

Running plays put the ball square in front of the uprights on the 6-yard line and, on fourth down, Jonas kicked a field goal from the 13.

An interception by Jim Schwab put the Lions at the Tech 11 on the first play after the next kickoff. Gursky and Torris carried to the goal line and Torris plunged over. Jonas converted.

Penn State coach Rip Engle, kneeling, poses with Nittany Lions standouts (left to right) Dave Robinson, Chuck Sieminski and Roger Kochman.

The Nittany Lions' Joe Galardi poses with Penn State's Gator Bowl trophy, and its 1961 Lambert Trophy, symbolic of the top Division I team in the East.

Pittsburgh 22 Penn State 21

THE RIP ENGLE ERA

Christmas Comes Early For Pitt as Panthers Edge Lions in Thriller

By Chester L. Smith

The Pittsburgh Press

The Pitt Panthers treated themselves to a pre-Christmas gift today at Pitt Stadium that has been a long, long time coming.

By defeating Penn State in a game that gushed with action from beginning to end, they wrapped up in a single package the district Big Three championship, a spot among the top three teams of the year nationally, the end of the Lions' three-season victory streak in the 70-year-old series and their own most artistic campaign (9-1) since 1937.

It was the first time since 1955 that the Jungle Cats had won over both Penn State and West Virginia. Old Ironsides, the hunk of steel that is symbolic of the area title, will now be a tenant in the Fitzgerald Field House for at least a year. Perhaps the Lions had a premonition of what was in store for them, for when their gear was trucked in from University Park Friday night, Old Ironsides was aboard. Now the weighty old gentleman won't have to make the return trip.

Penn State	7	7	7	0 —	21
Pittsburgh	0	12	3	7 —	22

This was a game that drove the sun-drenched crowd of 51,477 — almost the bowl's capacity — close to a case of mass hysterics.

Actually the margin for the Panthers was Rick Leeson's third-period, 35-yard field goal, but they could very well have been beaten in the waning moments when Ron Coates, the Lions kick specialist, missed for three points on a 37-yarder, which had ample distance but sliced off to the left.

For Pitt it was Freddie Mazurek running and passing, Leeson belting inside the tackles, a tremendous defensive effort by the alternate unit and all hands pitching in to help as the long season came to a happy end.

Touchdowns were traded at three apiece — Paul Martha, Leeson and

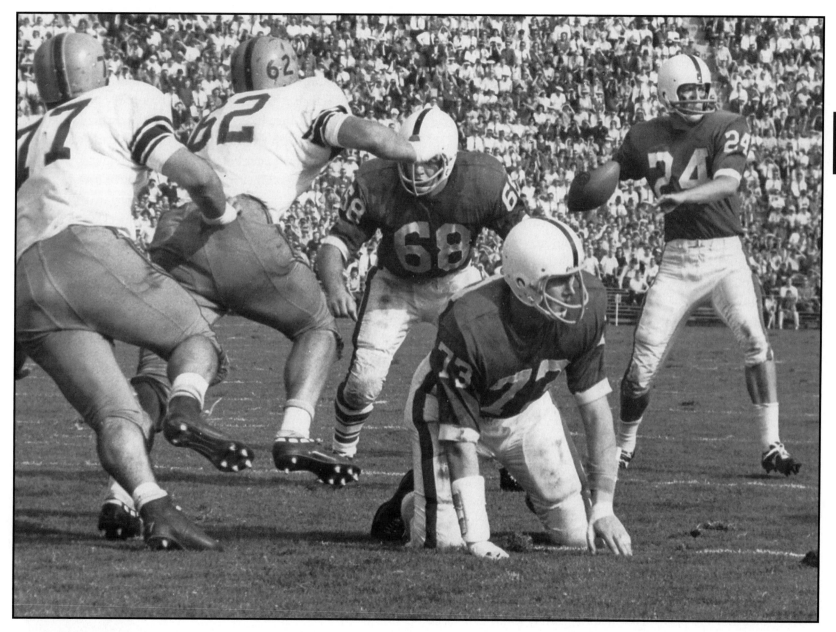

Penn State quarterback Pete Liske (24) threw for 1,117 yards and 10 touchdowns during the 1963 season, with the Lions finishing 7-3.

THE
RIP ENGLE
ERA

Mazurek scoring for Pitt; and Gary Klingensmith, Jerry Sandusky and Don Caum doing the honors for State.

After their first and second touchdowns, the Panthers tried for two points, but got none. On the initial touchdown, Mazurek was run out of bounds and his second attempt — a pass — wasn't close to anyone in particular. When the third score bobbed up, Leeson kicked for the single point and got it.

It was Mazurek's day by a landslide. The Redstone Raider not only carried in one six-pointer personally, but set up the two that preceded it with his good right arm and his ghost-like runs when he chose to leg it instead of pitch. Those legs scurried for 142 yards and he threw for another 108. The 250 yards total gave him a season's mark of 1,595. In the Miami game last week he had broken the school's total season offense high of 1,338 yards, set by Warren Heller in 1931.

In the voting that followed, Mazurek was the unanimous winner of the James H. Coogan Award, given each year in honor of the Lions' late public relations chief, to the game's most valuable player.

Overall, the Panthers were Penn State's masters by foot, but not by air. They outrushed their old friends from the mountains by 310 yards to 128, but were outgunned overhead by Pete Liske, 173 yards to 145. The total yardage was an impressive 421 yards for Pitt, 270 for the Lions.

The first hint that the Lions had come to Pittsburgh for something more than a weekend in the city came on the second play after the kickoff when Liske let fly with a fling to Caum from his own 21-yard line. The play had danger written all over it from the instant the Harrisburg senior gathered it in some 10 yards away and headed downfield.

There was a massive tangle of blockers and would-be tacklers in the neighborhood of Pitt's 30, but Caum escaped the trap and was away again, not to be caught until he was high-shouldered out of bounds at the 11 by Leeson.

A personal foul on a pass by Liske that went astray set the Lions back to their 29. Liske was able to get back only eight yards on a flip to Dick Anderson, but Coates missed on a field goal try from the 19.

But the touchdown that was denied State wasn't long in appearing … Ed Stuckrath, the day's defensive standout, blocked Tom Black's fourth-down punt and Bernie Sabol covered the ball on Pitt's 17.

Short punches by Klingensmith, Chris Weber and Stuckrath pushed the Panthers to their 9. Here, Liske, feinted beautifully on an apparent handoff to the right, then tucked the ball into Klingensmith's midriff as the latter slanted sharply leftward. The right halfback went across untouched, and seconds later Pitt was down seven points.

The Panthers were on their way to get six of them back before the quarter ended. This drive, for 96 yards, was highlighted by a fourth down gamble by Mazurek that had to be the most reckless of the fall.

On his own 45, Mazurak dropped back into kick formation, but instead sent Leeson straight ahead. Leeson swooped along for 34 yards to State's 21.

Staying on the ground, Mazurek, Martha and Leeson pounded away to the 4 but could go no farther.

Four plays later, Frank Hershey's punt rolled dead on his 46 and the Panthers were in gear once more.

Mazurek, Eric Crabtree and John Telesky rattled off a first down to the 32 and Mazurek went upstairs with a pair of passes to end Bill Howley good for 12 and 16 yards. Mazurek then ran to the Lions' 2 as the period ended.

Two plays after the interruption Pitt had its touchdown. Leeson needed only inches after his lunge and Martha measured it off — by inches.

The Panthers promptly countered a stroke of good fortune with a sour note

Quarterback Pete Liske threw for 173 yards against Pitt in 1963.

after they had kicked off. When Glenn Lehner intercepted a Liske pass, Pitt had the ball at its 37, but Mazurek's bobble, recovered by Ed Stewart gave the Lions immediate control on the 36.

They needed but seven plays to reach the end zone. Klingensmith and Weber swept to the 9 and Liske caught Sandusky behind the goal line with a high pass that called for a brilliant catch.

But back came the Panthers — for 80 yards and their second touchdown. Mazurek set the wheels to spinning with a 34-yard arching throw to Leeson. A holding foul cost 15 of those yards but Mazurek retrieved 16 by passing to Al Grigaliunas. Pitt then stayed earthbound for the remaining 43 yards.

Mazurek contributed 10- and 12-yard keepers, with Martha adding seven yards, and, from the 10, Leeson jamming to the 2. Leeson then hit for 1 yard. A penalty moved the ball a foot or so closer to the goal line. Afterward, Leeson plowed in for the touchdown.

A pass interference penalty of a Mazurek pass that started on the Pitt 32 and ended with the ball on Penn State's 30 gave the Panthers a chance to try for a field goal with seconds remaining in the half. Leeson kicked from the 37 but it was short.

Old Man Fumble belted the Panthers a second time shortly after the start of the second half. Mazurek lost the ball to Anderson at the 30 and the Lions prowled to the 9, where an offensive interference call sent them back to the 25. Liske threw to Joe Vargo but for not enough, and Pitt had the ball on the 12.

The events leading up to the all-important field goal now began to unroll. Mazurek turned himself loose from his 22 and he was 42 yards away on Penn State's 36 when he was overtaken and grounded by Anderson.

When the mob was unpiled, Mazurek didn't get up and the Pitt segment of the crowd moaned when he wobbled to the bench and was replaced by Kenny Lucas.

However, the Glassport sophomore used Leeson and Bodle to reel off a first down on the 21, passed to Joe Kuzneski on the 10 and appeared to be in full command of the situation when he was stabbed for a 10-yard loss by Stuckrath.

That put Leeson in the field goal kicking role that was to mean the victory.

But it didn't seem that way when the Lions responded to the challenge with a 74-yard stampede that didn't end until Liske had passed the last 10 yards to Caum for the third touchdown. The key plays that came before were Liske's 16-yard shot to Klingensmith, Weber's 30-yard sprint through the middle on Penn State's famed scissors, and a 14-yarder to Caum that planted the ball on the 9.

The Panthers now picked up the baton and were off and running. They opened from their 23 and were midfield, largely on a Lucas to Crabtree pass that was good for 25 yards as the third quarter closed out.

Mazurek returned for the final period and promptly risked disaster with a fourth-down toss of the dice. He got away with it, fired a pass to Bodle for 11 yards and raced seven more to Penn State's 21.

Bodle chipped in with another four yards, and the Redstone Raider, with an option to pitch or prance, saw an alley open to his right. Down it he scrambled for the 17 yards that were left — and the scoring for the day was over.

But not the suspense. Before the finish, the Lions took over on downs on their own 47 when Pitt misfired on a fourth-down punt attempt, and an exchange of punts left the Lions on their 42.

Pass interference on Caum swept them along to Pitt's 42. There Liske passed to Klingensmith at the 26 and to Anderson on the 22. But there was more yardage left than they cared to risk and Coates tried for his win-or-go-broke field goal. Broke was the answer.

All the Panthers needed at this point was a first down to allow them to retain the ball and as a parting gesture for the season. Mazurek did the trick with a twisting run of 27 yards. He ate the ball on the last play.

Penn State 27 Ohio State 0

November 7, 1964 | Columbus, Ohio

Lions Pile It On in Rout of No. 2-Ranked Ohio State

By Lester J. Biederman

The Pittsburgh Press

Penn State not only rubbed much of the gloss and glamour off previously undefeated, No. 2 Ohio State today, but made its 27-0 victory look ridiculously easy.

The Lions roared for the full 60 minutes this bright sunny afternoon and not only mystified the Buckeyes but also most of the 84,279 fans who had attended the weekly ritual at Ohio Stadium.The performance of the Lions was unbelievably good and they, in turn, made the Bucks look unbelievably bad. Watching the game today, it was difficult to visualize the Ohio State as undefeated and Penn State with a 3-4 record before the game.

The only bright spot in an otherwise exceedingly dull day for Ohio State was the defeat of Purdue by Michigan State, leaving the Buckeyes the only unbeaten team in the Big Ten.

Penn State completely dominated the game from start to finish.

The Lions scored a touchdown in every quarter, had numerous other chances, and never allowed the Buckeyes to touch Penn State territory

Penn State	7	7	6	7 —	27
Ohio State	0	0	0	0 —	0

until the final futile minutes.

The Lions were two touchdown underdogs but they proceeded to not only pile up four TD's but to hold Ohio State scoreless for the first time since 1959, when the Buckeyes and Indiana played a scoreless contest.

The Lions won everything. Their supreme effort of the season was overwhelmingly displayed in the statistics.

Penn State had 22 first downs to only five for Ohio. The Lions piled up 201 yards rushing. The Buckeyes, who specialize in ball control and rushing, had the ball only 23 times for rushes and gained but 33 yards.

The Bucks netted just two yards rushing the first quarter and wound up a minus-14 yards for the first half.

Penn State's 1964 upset of No. 2 Ohio State made Nittany Lions players such as Glenn Ressler popular targets for autograph hunters. Penn State shocked Ohio State, 27-0, in the teams' 1964 meeting.

Penn State assistant coach George Welsh pores over some notes during a 1964 road trip.

Gary Wydman, in his best day of the season, completed 12 of 22 passes for 148 yards and didn't have one intercepted. The Bucks' Don Unverferth completed just three in 14 and had two intercepted.

Penn State went in for the touchdown kill on four reasonably long marches. The first two covered 65 yards each, the third 41 yards and the final trip to paydirt was 63 yards long.

Wydman turned magician with an amazing display of ball handling.

On the first touchdown cruise, he hit Don Kunit with a pass in the flat that was good for 35 yards and perched the Lions on the Buckeyes' 11-yard line.

Bob Riggle wriggled through the middle for seven yards and, on third down, Tom Urbanik fled through the line for an apparent touchdown but fumbled as he tumbled into the end zone.

Fortunately, Dirk Nye was there to fall on the ball ahead of two Buckeyes and Penn State had six points. Gerry Sanker tacked on the extra point and with 8:24 gone, the Lions had a 7-0 lead that was to grow and grow and grow.

Sanker missed a field goal from the 10-yard line at the start of the second period, but the Lions came pounding back on a 65-yard march for a TD.

Wydman passed 11 yards to Bill Bowes, Urbanik charged straight ahead for 18 and before anybody realized it, Penn State was perched on the OSU 3-yard line.

Wydman went back to pass, decided to run and raced around his left end for the three yards and the score. Sanker again made the kick good for a 14-0 Penn State lead.

Penn State was deep in Ohio State territory twice more before the half ended, but nothing came of it.

The Lions lost the ball on the Ohio State 15 when a fourth-down plunge failed by inches early in the third quarter, but this merely delayed them.

Dick Gingrich intercepted a pass on the Buckeyes' 41 and Wydman went to work again. He passed 12 yards to Riggle, 12 more to Bill Huber

Fullback Tom Urbanik led Penn State's 1964 team in rushing, compiling 625 yards and scoring eight touchdowns.

and then Kunit and Urbanik carried the ball.

Kunit took it over with a two-yard sprint around his left and this time Sanker's kick was wide but Penn State had a 20-0 lead.

The Buckeyes, looking worse every minute, finally chalked up a first down in the final seconds of the third quarter on two consecutive passes.

But the Lion had one mighty roar left and, with nine minutes remaining in the game, they ran and passed 63 yards in 10 plays for the final touchdown.

Urbanik ripped off 13 yards up the middle and Gary Klingensmith ran like a man on fire. Klingensmith sprinted for eight yards and kept on fighting for extra yardage.

Then Kunit and Dave McNaughton took over. Kunit turned his left end for 12 yards, McNaughton added seven over the middle and Kunit tore around his left end for the last five yards.

Sanker's kick was true and the Penn State lead rose to 27-0 and the Buckeye diehards began to leave the stadium.

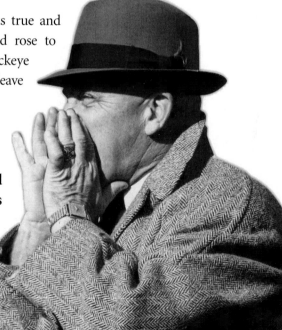

Rip Engle served as Penn State's head coach from 1950-1965. His record was 104-48-4.

THE RIP ENGLE ERA

65

THE JOE PATERNO ERA

"I told our kids at halftime that I didn't care if we won or lost, but that they would find out something about themselves as men in the second half."

JOE PATERNO

Penn State 17 Miami 8

September 29, 1967 | Miami, Fla.

Penn State Blows Past Hurricanes, Just Missing a Shutout

JOE
PATERNO
ERA

By Roy McHugh

The Pittsburgh Press

Charlie Tate, Miami's head football coach, put it all together last night after losing to Penn State in the Orange Bowl, 17-8.

"Their defense was stronger than I expected," he said.

It was stronger than anybody expected.

Non-existent against Navy a week ago, Penn State's defense had Miami shut out with 47 seconds to play. This made it very difficult for Miami to substantiate the betting odds that made the Hurricanes an 11-point favorite.

The first quarter, which was scoreless, decided the game. Miami made a first down on the 9-yard line and could get no farther. Then a fumble gave Miami the ball on the 35 and again nothing happened except a second missed field–goal attempt by Ray Harris.

Joe Paterno's young Lions — six sophomores were playing on the defensive unit, three of them 18-year-olds — now perceived that they were not going to be run out of the stadium.

| Penn State | 0 | 6 | 8 | 3 — | 17 |
| Miami | 0 | 0 | 0 | 8 — | 8 |

After that, with each minute that went by, Penn State's defense became harder to move and Miami's offense became easier to stop.

And the initiative switched to the Lions. After missing two field-goal attempts, from slightly beyond Don Abbey's range, they missed a first down on Miami's 1-yard line and then put an end to the stuttering.

Late in the second quarter, Bob Campbell zig-zagged through Miami for a 50-yard run. On the next play, from Miami's 15, quarterback Tom Sherman threw a touchdown pass to Ted Kwalick, alone in the end zone.

The Lions thus completed a 90-yard drive and, though Abbey missed the extra point, their troubles were over.

They put on another drive in the third quarter, this time going 59

JOE
PATERNO
ERA

Tom Sherman (right) threw 2 touchdown passes against Miami.

yards with Sherman passing to Abbey from the 7 for the touchdown.

A two-point conversion on a pass to Jack Curry and Abbey's fourth-quarter field goal from 24 yards put the Lions so far ahead that Miami's fair-weather friends in the crowd of 39,516 started heading for home.

As time ran out, Miami got down to the Penn State 3, but Neal Smith, a non-scholarship sophomore in the Lions' defensive backfield, broke up two passes in the end zone.

Miami wasn't going to score, it appeared. Then, on fourth down at the Penn State 17, Campbell, back to punt, saw he was not being rushed, decided to run, changed his mind about a yard from the line of scrimmage and tried to kick on the move. The ball squirted off his foot and Miami had it.

Bill Miller at once threw a 24-yard touchdown pass to Jimmy Cox.

Earlier, both Miller and Miami's other quarterback, Dave Olivo, had been missing their receivers and Miami's running attack got the Hurricanes nowhere.

Vince Opalsky, the sophomore from McKeesport who ran for close to 100 yards against Northwestern last week, gained 9 yards and no one else was much better.

After Campbell's long run, a scissors play on which he changed directions when his blockers weren't where he thought they'd be, the Lions found it easy to run on Miami. Sherman completed 15 of 24 passes and mixed up his plays well.

When Penn State lost to Navy and with Miami and UCLA coming up, it seemed that the Lions would be off to an 0-3 start. Now they are 1-1 and everybody is wondering how Miami, 0-2, could have been rated so highly in the preseason forecasts.

**Ted Kwalick (82) scored the Lions' first touchdown
with a 15-yard reception, alone in the end zone.**

Penn State 17 Florida State 17

December 30, 1967 | Jacksonville, Fla.

Florida State Rallies in Fourth Quarter To Tie Lions

By Roy McHugh

The Pittsburgh Press

Penn State gambled and tied in the Gator Bowl yesterday. On their own 15-yard line, 17 points ahead in the third quarter, the Lions tried a fourth-down quarterback sneak. Within the next minute, Florida State had two touchdowns — not one touchdown, but two — and when Grant Guthrie kicked a 26-yard field goal 15 seconds before the end of the game, it all came out even, 17-17.

"I blew it," said Joe Paterno, Penn State's coach, "I've been around football long enough to know better."

But the night before, Paterno had said the Lions were going to have some fun. This they did.

Paterno changed his lineup around to stymie Florida State's passing game and to get a little more mileage out of Ted Kwalick, the all–American tight end.

He used offensive and defensive formations the Lions never had tried before. And for two quarters, he looked like a genius.

Penn State	3	14	0	0 —	17
Florida State	0	0	14	3 —	17

Kwalick, acclaimed as the best tight end in the country, played wingback. "We had to get the ball to Kwalick to win," Paterno said, but one of those times a touchdown resulted.

From some crazy formations, including one that resembled a "Y," tailback Charlie Pittman ran for 128 yards. And on defense, the Lions had three men playing new positions and Tim Montgomery "roaming the outfield" — all in the interest of greater quickness.

Kim Hammond, Florida State's quarterback, set Gator Bowl records for passes completed (37) and passing yardage (362) and Ron Sellers, the split end, caught 14 of Hammond's passes for still another Gator Bowl record, but Penn State prevented them from executing their trademark play, the long bomb.

And at halftime, the Lions led by two touchdowns and a field goal. The record Gator Bowl crowd of 68,019 had nothing left to enjoy but the bright, balmy weather.

Then the third quarter started and so did Florida State. Presently, the Seminoles had a first down on the 3-yard line. But Penn State held as Jim Kates, the new middle guard, stopped a quarterback sneak from inside the 1 and Jim Litterelle chopped Hammond down on the 5 as he attempted a rollout.

The Lions got out to the 15, with one foot to go on fourth down — and it happened.

Tom Sherman bucked straight ahead and the Florida State line hardly budged.

"The kids wanted to try it," said Paterno "and I didn't think anybody could stop a sneak on us."

According to Sherman, nobody did.

"I went up Lenkaitis' back," he said (Bill Lenkaitis is the Penn State center), "and I was over the 15-yard line. Then someone grabbed me by the seat of the pants and pulled me back."

Paterno said: "It was a very debatable call until I see the movies."

Anyway, it was now Florida State's ball, and two plays later Hammond passed 15 yards to Sellers for a touchdown, Sellers taking the ball on the 5 and dodging across the goal line.

Guthrie converted, Florida State kicked off and immediately afterward the Seminoles had the ball again. The kickoff went to Pittman, Mike Blatt jarred him into a fumble and Chuck Elliott recovered for Florida State on the Penn State 22.

A screen pass — Hammond to Bill Mooreman — put the Seminoles inside the 1, and this time Hammond's sneak made the end zone.

Penn State's offense, in the second half, produced only one first down and it came with three minutes left in the fourth quarter. Dan Lucyk gained two yards off tackle, enabling Penn State to keep the ball for another minute and a half. But when a third-and-five sweep by Pittman gained one yard less than the Lions needed, they had to punt, and

JOE PATERNO ERA

Penn State quarterback Tom Sherman (25) loses the ball after a hard hit from Florida State's Floyd Ratliff during the 1967 Gator Bowl.

Hammond passed Florida State right down the field.

First, though, he burst through the middle for 21 yards.

Fighting the clock, the Seminoles lined up without a huddle. Hammond passed 13 yards to Lane Fenner, 12 to Moreman for a first down on the 13 and five more to Fenner, who fell out of bounds on the Lions' 8.

Then Hammond overthrew Moreman and Penn State's Bob Capretto saved a touchdown by knocking the ball out of Sellers' hands in the end zone.

So Guthrie came in and kicked a field goal.

Florida State coach Bill Peterson explained why he went for a tie.

"If we were the ones who were 17 points ahead, I'd have gone for the win," he said. "But the way we came back, I felt I couldn't throw it away."

Sherman had opened the scoring for Penn State with a field goal from the 27 in the first quarter. In the second quarter, he missed one from the 31, but Florida State was offside and Sherman got a touchdown out of it by passing to Jack Curry in the corner of the end zone on a play good for nine yards.

Then in the last two minutes of the half, Penn State drove 82 yards for a touchdown. Pittman ran 36 on a draw play, but it was Sherman himself who kept the Lions going. Blitzed on fourth down at the Florida State 27, he got away from four tacklers and scrambled down to the 12.

On the next play, after faking to Lucyk, he passed to Kwalick alone in the end zone.

Thus, two of the seven passes Sherman completed went for touchdowns. Hammond threw 53 times (another Gator Bowl record) for his 37 completions.

Penn State had four interceptions and got to Hammond several times behind the line of scrimmage, with Frank Spaziani, Neal Smith and Steve Smear leading the rush.

"I said if we could get four interceptions and throw Hammond for four losses, we'd win," Paterno reflected. "Obviously, I wasn't right."

Don Abbey, the Lions' injured sophomore fullback, did not get into

Nittany Lions running back Bob Campbell looks for running room.

Penn State defender Neal Smith (26) looks to break up a second-quarter pass intended for Florida State's Bill Gunter (31). After taking a 17-0 lead in the first half, Smith and his teammates saw the Seminoles score 17 points in the second half.

JOE
PATERNO
ERA

the game, even for a field goal attempt, but Bob Campbell was in uniform for the first time since a knee operation in October. He did the punting for Penn State.

One of his punts went 68 yards over the safety man's head and gave the Lions a breathing spell in the fourth quarter.

Paterno, who had held secret practices for 10 days before the game, said "the changes we made were great. They really helped us, but Florida State did a great job of adjusting at halftime.

"I was pleased with the way we took the bomb away from them, though they had one and didn't hang onto it."

Sellers, in the clear once, dropped a pass when Capretto came up

from behind. Later, Hammond overthrew Sellers when Sellers was free for a touchdown catch.

"This is a funny ball club," Paterno said. "I don't know how to put my finger on it, but we get ahead and get tight. We get a little bit cautious."

The Lions won most of their games this season — they had an 8-2 record — by jumping off to an early lead and then surviving.

Someone asked Paterno about the rumor that the New York Jets want him to be their new coach.

"After the fourth-and-one call," he said, "I may not be coaching anywhere next year."

It was only an exit line, and not a bad one.

Penn State 15 Kansas 14

January 1, 1969 | Miami, Fla.

12th Man Boosts 'Dead' Lions in Orange Bowl Victory

By Roy McHugh

The Pittsburgh Press

Two minutes to play on a moonless Miami night in the Orange Bowl. Kansas had the ball. Kansas had a first down. Kansas had a seven–point lead. There was no way Penn State could win.

Over the public-address system in the press box came the announcement that seemed to make it final: "Most Valuable player — Donnie Shanklin of Kansas."

There was no way Penn State would win, but Penn State won.

Penn State won, 15-14, on Chuck Burkhart's touchdown run in the closing seconds and Bob Campbell's run for a two-point conversion after Kansas had given the Lions a second chance.

The last two minutes were pure, unadulterated insanity.

It really started with Mike Reid, the toughest piano player in Altoona, Pa., bounding through the Kansas defense and dropping Jayhawk quarterback Bobby Douglass for a six-yard loss on second down. Situation still hopeless. But Penn State called a time out, stopping the clock.

Penn State	3	14	0	0 —	17
Florida State	0	0	14	3 —	17

Then here was Reid again, after Douglass and spilling him for a seven-yard loss. Another time out and now Kansas was punting from its 25-yard line.

In rushed Neal Smith from his safety position to get a hand on the ball as it left the kicker's foot. The punt slanted off to the left and bounced to the Penn State 49-yard line.

Penn State had a minute 16 seconds and it obviously wouldn't be enough, for Kansas had been stopping the Lions cold.

Only this time the play was "One Go." On "One Go," Burkhart goes back with the ball and Campbell goes straight down the field. As Burkhart went back, the Kansas pass rush came — but not before Burkhart threw.

Kansas fans celebrate after the Jayhawks stopped Penn State's potential game-winning two-point conversion, but the celebration turned out to be premature. An official holds up a penalty flag, signalling that Kansas has 12 men on the field for the play.

The ball came down between two defensive backs and right into Campbell's arms on the Kansas 20. Campbell stumbled forward. The Kansas backs stumbled after him, and he fell on the 3.

Penn State's last time out stopped the clock with 66 seconds left. Then it was Tom Cherry into the line for no gain and Cherry again into the line for no gain. Without a huddle, the Lions got over the ball.

Burkhart, taking the snap, faked to Don Abbey, then he faked to

Charlie Pittman. Finally, all by himself, Burkhart rolled to his left and into the end zone untouched.

With fifteen seconds left, 14-13, there was no doubt what Penn State would do — go for two points, play to win. Burkhart rolled out and passed, but too high for Ted Kwalick's desperate leap.

The Kansas band was on the field, Kansas rooters in the crowd of 77,000 were pouring down from the stands. And the officials were ges-

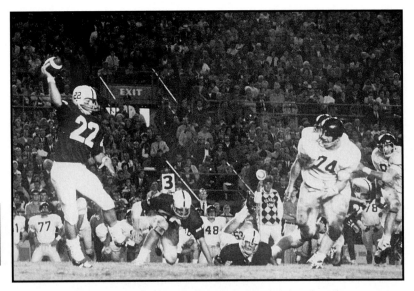

Penn State quarterback Chuck Burkhart (22) completed 12 passes for 154 yards.

It's official — State's Ted Kwalick, left, and Dennis Onkotz were 1968 all-Americans.

turing wildly, holding up their hands and pointing to a flag on the goal line.

Kansas had stopped the conversion try with 12 men, which no matter how you count it, is one too many. Suddenly, pandemonium sets in.

The penalty moved the ball from the 3 to inside the 2. And this time it was no pass, it was Campbell sweeping to his left, hurling himself over the goal line as Cherry took out the cornerback and Charlie Zapiec took out the all-American Kansas end, John Zook.

On the clock, it said 15 seconds.

When the clock was down to zero, on the first play after Penn State's kickoff, Steve Smear had a death grip on the 6-foot-4 Douglass and the Lions had topped off an undefeated season, making 19 games since the last time anyone beat them.

"To be honest," said Reid in the locker room, "I don't know how we won this one."

In the first quarter, Penn State had given the ball to Kansas three times — on two interceptions and a fumble — and, after the second interception, Kansas running the ball nine times, drove 45 yards to a touchdown, with Mike Reeves scoring from the 2.

Before the half was over, Penn State tied at 7-7 in much the same way, going 47 yards in six plays, all on the ground. The touchdown came on a 13-yard trap, Pittman up the middle undeterred.

Penn State finished the half outgaining Kansas by a 2-1 margin, Campbell alone running for 93 yards, but the score was still 7-7.

Once when Douglass passed from his 9-yard line with Smear wrapped around his ankles, Dennis Onkotz deflected the ball and Mike Smith intercepted it, making a 23-yard runback to the 11. At the 6, however, Cherry fumbled and then, on the last play of the half, Rusty Garthwaite missed a 31-yard field goal attempt.

The third quarter started with Burkhart completing three straight third-down passes and moving Penn State to the Kansas 5. There the underrated Kansas line yielded only four and a half yards to Cherry in three carries. Then Emory Hicks, a linebacker, shot through to nail

Penn State's Charlie Pittman (left) finished with 58 yards rushing and two receptions.

Pittman on the 2 and the ball belonged to Kansas.

Douglass, running and passing, got field position for Kansas early in the fourth quarter. Penn State had to punt from its 14 and Shanklin, winning his premature MVP spurs, returned the ball 46 yards to the 7.

Two plays later, John Riggins bolted across from the 1.

As time passed, and Penn State did nothing, it looked like the end. But it wasn't.

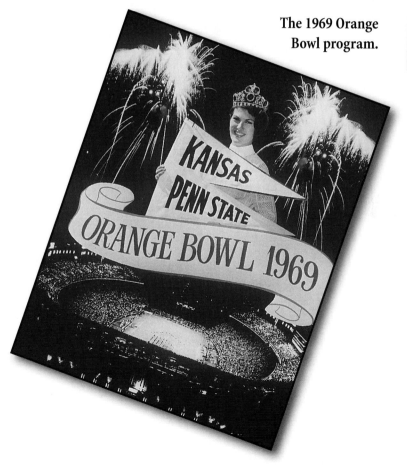

The 1969 Orange Bowl program.

Penn State 15 Syracuse 14

October 18, 1969 | Syracuse, N.Y.

Inspired Nittany Lions Rally to Defeat Syracuse

By Phil Musick

The Pittsburgh Press

Penn State	0	0	0	15 —	15
Syracuse	7	7	0	0 —	14

Agreat football team beat a good football team on a bad day, and everyone agreed — as a character builder — Joe Paterno has few peers.

After giving a classic performance yesterday of the old, old football exercise — "sucking in your guts" — the Nittany Lions to a man pointed to pride as the raison d'etre for Syracuse's sudden and unexpected demise before a record Homecoming crowd of 42,291 that really didn't believe what it saw.

When it was over and Penn State had jammed 15 points into a hectic 3:17 of the fourth quarter to whip the inspired Orangemen, 15-14, the fans stood and gave Coach Ben Schwartzwalder's dead-game troops a standing ovation.

Paterno would have stood and applauded too had he not been in the Lions' dressing room and drinking deeply of the sweet, sweet essence of victory.

"I wish someone would say how great our football team really is," he said of his Lions, who made Syracuse their 16th consecutive victim and protected the nation's longest non-losing streak — 24 games.

"When you beat a good football team on a bad day you're great. They were awful strong … awful strong."

Craggy old Archbold Stadium — a concrete inner-city bowl that leaves you expecting the Christians vs. the Lions at any moment — hummed from beginning to end.

Punt returns of 61, 46 and 46 yards by a sophomore back who Schwartzwalder says "always runs out of gas," Greg Allen, allowed the Orange to completely dominate the first half.

But the Nittany Lions' character came to the fore in the final two quarters, along with a defensive effort that finally turned off Syracuse's

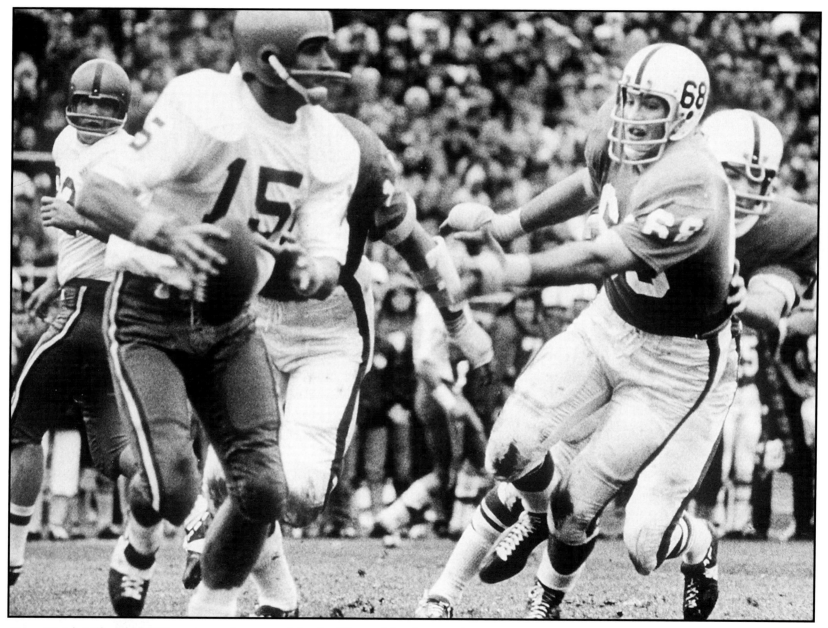

Penn State's Mike Reid (68) puts on a heavy rush in the Nittany Lions' 15-14 victory over Syracuse in 1969.

JOE
PATERNO
ERA

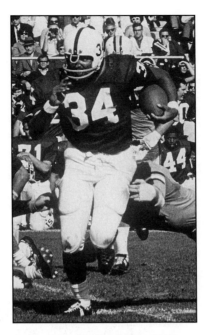

Lydell Mitchell, left, led Penn State in rushing in both the 1970 and 1971 seasons, and finished with 2,934 career yards. Franco Harris, right, had five 100-yard rushing games during his career.

electrifying attack.

"I told our kids at halftime that I didn't care if we won or lost, but that they would find out something about themselves as men in the second half," Paterno said. Knute Rockne, himself, couldn't have said it better.

Inspired, the Lions took it to Syracuse in the fourth quarter after being totally stymied in the first three periods and being down, 14-0, going into the last 15 minutes.

"I was really worried if we could ever move the ball on them," Paterno admitted after Penn State had won its third straight Homecoming encounter and handed Syracuse its second loss in five games. "We practiced all week on the big play."

That practice paid a dividend in the fourth quarter when sophomore fullback Franco Harris roared through a block by guard Charlie Zapiec

and outran a Syracuse defender 36 yards for the touchdown that tied the game, 14-14. Mike Reitz's extra point untied it and Penn State's hopes for its second straight undefeated season received a shot in the arm.

"A run like that's instinctive," said Harris, who went all the way at fullback because of an injury that benched veteran Don Abbey. "We never lost confidence, we knew what we could do in the clutch."

What Penn State could do in the clutch became apparent with 10:18 remaining to play when a Lions defense that had been embarrassed all afternoon came alive with a vengeance as linebacker Jack Ham recovered an Al Newton fumble at the Orange 32.

Seven plays later, a pass interference penalty against Syracuse safety Don Dorr gave the Lions the ball at the Orange 4-yard line. On the next play Lydell Mitchell rammed over for the touchdown that gave Lions fans some hope. It even gave Paterno hope.

"It was in my mind that we had to get the big play," Paterno said. "We had to get momentum and I knew we couldn't ram one down their throats."

The imperturbable Penn State defense was willing to try, however, and stiffened Syracuse on three straight plays in the series following the Lions' first touchdown.

Syracuse punted, Harris hit for a yard to the Orange 36 and then made a bit of philosophy by Zapiec stand up when he burst away for the touchdown that tied it with 7:01 left to play.

Legendary Lions: Lydell Mitchell (23), Lenny Moore and Charlie Pittman (24).

JOE PATERNO ERA

"If we couldn't have won this kind of a game, we couldn't have had a great season," said Zapiec. "We'll remember this one for a long time."

Harris will, indeed, remember it for a long time. His two-point run for the conversion after the Penn State touchdown was pivotal and came after he failed on a previous attempt, getting a second chance due to a Syracuse penalty.

Among other things, it gave rise to a feeling, not shared by Paterno, that it's all downhill from Syracuse for the Lions, who face lightweights such as Ohio U., Boston College and Pitt in their final five games.

The first of Syracuse's three interceptions set up the Orangemen's first touchdown, as Gary Bletch returned a Chuck Burkhart pass 32 yards to the Lions 24. Tailback Ron Trask got 13 yards to the 8-yard line and Newton punched over from a yard out.

Again, Allen streaked away on a punt, this time taking one 46 yards as Syracuse set up shop on the Lions 6-yard line with only :45 gone in the second quarter. Quarterback Randy Zur then rolled wide to his right and cut back for six yards and Syracuse's second touchdown.

But the Orange blew a third scoring opportunity when Allen carried his third punt reception 46 yards to the Penn State 29. A minute later, on a fourth-and-one play from the Lions 3, Allen fell down on a sweep.

"That was the key play," said Paterno. "It kept us in the game. It would have been very rough getting 21 points back with them fired up like that."

Above, Charlie Pittman (24), who led Penn State with 706 yards rushing in 1969, turns the corner; Below, Penn State's 1969 starting offensive unit poses for a group shot; Bottom left, Pittman and Mike Reid (right) were named all-Americans.

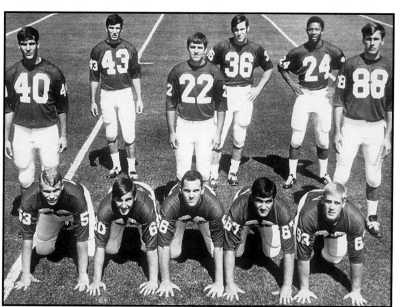

83

Penn State 10 Missouri 3

January 1, 1970 | Miami, Fla.

Burkhart Has Last Laugh on Missouri in Orange Bowl Win

By Phil Musick

The Pittsburgh Press

Exit Chuck Burkhart ... laughing. He stood there in front of his locker, sticking out a hairless chest defiantly, and his catfish grin told it all: "Yeah, you boobs," it snickered, "you don't believe it, do you."

Chuck Burkhart, Penn State's "poor soul," the kid who could "only" win, was the 36th Orange Bowl's most valuable back. Uneasy reporters, who had mocked his talents, were Burkhart's delight.

Forcing nine turnovers — seven on pass interceptions — Penn State made powderkeg Missouri victim No. 30, 10-3, but the most brilliant defensive effort in the school's history was saved by a Burkhart offensive effort.

For probably the first time in his life, Burkhart was cocky. He completed 11 of 26 passes for 187 yards and the only touchdown in a game that saw Penn State's defense simply overpower and out-talent Missouri's quicksilver offense.

"A couple of more games and we'll get the Big Eight title," crowed

| Penn State | 10 | 0 | 0 | 0 — | 10 |
| Missouri | 0 | 3 | 0 | 0 — | 3 |

Burkhart to the unbelievers, who finally had to believe.

The Lions' 22nd straight win, third this year over a Big Eight foe, was heady stuff. "Yeah, I'd like to try the pro's," Burkhart laughed. Not a writer blinked; no one sneered. Best of all, the pros like a winner.

The explanations for Penn State's triumph over a team that had averaged 36 points a game fell like the rain that drenched a record crowd of 78,282 during the second half.

But perhaps the most pertinent one came earlier in the week when Lions assistant coach Frank Patrick said of Missouri quarterback Terry McMillan, "he throws long and he throws high. I like the high part."

McMillan, manhandled by Penn State defensive tackles Steve Smear and Mike Reid, the game's most valuable lineman, threw more intercep-

Penn State's defense gave up 306 total yards in the 1970 Orange Bowl, but allowed only three points and forced nine Missouri turnovers, including seven pass interceptions.

Penn State's Lydell Mitchell (23) scores the only touchdown of the 1970 Orange Bowl, a 28-yard pass from Chuck Burkhart that got past Missouri's Lorenzo Brinkley.

tions (five) than completions (four).

The seven pass thefts set an Orange Bowl record and scotched the five Missouri drives that had reached Penn State territory.

"That's the best secondary ever put together," said Lions defensive boss Jim O'Hora, after backs George Landis and Neal Smith and linebacker Denny Onkotz had each picked off two Tigers passes. The other Penn State interception was made by end Gary Hull.

"How could any team in the country be better than Penn State?" asked Missouri coach Dan Devine, who had no excuses and few explanations.

"Terry wouldn't want any excuses and I don't either," Devine said. "We couldn't block Smear and Reid. They got in there and got the job done. I did a poor job preparing my team in so many ways, I couldn't be specific."

Devine wouldn't elaborate and McMillan, shaken up in the second quarter by Reid, sat over in a corner crying.

His replacement, junior Chuck Roper, knew how he felt. Roper threw

two interceptions himself and the last one, by Landis with 53 seconds to play, proved that the Penn State defense wasn't too whipped to do it — as a school official cried — "one more time."

Missouri, held to a 35-yard field goal by Henry Brown with 1:56 to go in the second quarter, gasped out one final drive in the final two minutes on a pair of Roper-to-end-John Henley passes for 10 and 33 yards, but Landis, hobbled by a knee injury, was equal to the test.

The red-haired junior, who blanked one of Missouri's most potent weapons, end Mel Gray, stole a pass for Henley at the Lions 3 and returned it to the Tigers' 42.

Smoke bombs burst on the field and thousands of youngsters roared on to the soggy Orange Bowl turf. They knew it was over, but Burkhart had to kill a minute with four sneaks to prove it to the officials.

Missouri's best weapons in the first half were punt returns of 47 and 48 yards by Jon Staggers, and the Tigers got to the Lions' 26, 47, 7, 18 and 8 only to have Reid put them back in the bag.

Missouri tried to contain the all-America tackle with another all-American, offensive tackle Mike Carroll, but Carroll wasn't quite ready for Reid, who forced three Tiger turnovers in the first half and another in the third quarter.

The game began in 75-degree temperatures and Missouri immediately picked up momentum behind Staggers' power sweeps.

But Brown missed a 47-yard field goal try on the Tigers' first series. On the following series, the Lions' Mike Reitz drilled home a 29-yard field goal to put Penn State on the board with 3:42 remaining in the opening quarter.

On Missouri's first play from scrimmage following the Lions kickoff, Reid racked Tigers fullback Joe Moore and linebacker Mike Smith recovered the first of Missouri's four fumbles at the losers' 28.

Burkhart, who had lost a contact lens on the prior series, rolled out and threw to halfback Lydell Mitchell for the game's only touchdown. "I probably throw better without it," grinned Burkhart.

Mitchell's score, set up by tight end Pete Johnson's crackback block, made it 10-0, with 3:23 to play in the period.

Staggers returned a Penn State punt 64 yards in the final minute of the second quarter, but Reid blew in on McMillan and his wobbly pass was snatched by Hull.

Burkhart, who was dropped for 76 yards in losses, faltered briefly in the second quarter, throwing an interception, but Missouri couldn't capitalize on it.

"I always thought Burkhart was a great passer, but we never gave him an opportunity like we did tonight," said Penn State coach Joe Paterno, who told a few reporters yesterday morning that Penn State would pass "at least 20 times," and "couldn't run outside."

Landis intercepted at the Missouri 34 midway in the quarter, but Penn State was forced to punt. McMillan then ran 30 yards to set the Tigers up at the Penn State 9. But, on a reverse, Lions end John Ebersole stripped Gray of the ball and recovered it at the 22 to end that threat.

Staggers' second sprint with a punt later put Missouri in possession at the Penn State 18, but Reid shook off Carroll to rip McMillan, and Onkotz swiped a pass at the 4.

Late in the first half, Missouri parlayed a 40-yard pass from McMillan to Moore and some shifty inside running by Staggers to move 85 yards to the Penn State 8-yard line.

But Reid and Smear dumped McMillan back on the 17 and Missouri settled for Brown's field goal to make it 10-3.

That was it, Neal Smith picked off his 11th and 12th interceptions in the second half and Onkotz and Landis each got a second steal.

Missouri tried a 52-yard field goal that missed early in the final quarter, after Penn State blew one from the 18 with just 2:50 into the period.

Burkhart set it up with a throw to Pete Johnson for 56 yards, but two

Linebacker Dennis Onkotz (35) intercepted two passes against Missouri — as did Penn State teammates George Landis and Neal Smith.

straight offensive penalties checked the drive. When Charlie Pittman was stopped at the 1-yard line, Paterno elected to try the field goal.

"A field goal wins it," said Paterno. "I didn't want to do the same thing we did last year down here." Penn State beat Kansas, 15-14, in the 1969 classic on a last-second touchdown scamper by … uh … Burkhart.

Would Penn State be No. 1 nationally when the final tally is made?

"I'm up to my ears in polls — I'm tired of the controversy," said Paterno.

"People said I was sour grapes, that I shot off my mouth. But I was willing to go out on a limb for my kids. Maybe we're not the best, but how could anyone be better?"

Don't worry about it, Joe. Everybody said Burkhart couldn't pass, too.

JOE
PATERNO
ERA

Penn State 30 Texas 6

January 1, 1972 | Dallas, Tex.

Penn State Explodes in 2nd Half, Rips Longhorns

By Phil Musick

The Pittsburgh Press

Penn State, trailing by 6-3 at halftime, broke loose for 17 points in the third quarter and went on to butcher Texas in the Cotton Bowl yesterday.

Lydell Mitchell and John Hufnagel led the Lions' second-half charge as the Penn State defense stopped the Longhorns in their tracks.

Penn State survived the vaunted Texas wishbone on the Longhorns' first offensive series. Texas drove to the Penn State 30, but quarterback Eddie Phillips was trapped for losses on two straight plays and the Longhorns punted, downing the ball at the Lions 2-yard line.

Penn State couldn't move the ball and a 28-yard punt by Bob Parsons gave Texas excellent field position at the Lions 35 and it was worth three points.

The Longhorns moved to the 19, but Phillips lost a yard and threw an incomplete pass and, with 1:14 to play in the first quarter, Steve Valek kicked a 29-yard field goal to give Texas a 3-0 lead.

Penn State	0	3	17	10 —	30
Texas	3	3	0	0 —	6

The wishbone snapped the next time Texas had the ball. Fullback Dennis Ladd was racked up by linebackers John Skorupan and Tom Hull at the Longhorn's 20 and fumbled the ball into the hands of defensive halfback Chuck Mesko.

Penn State, with Mitchell getting yardage off tackle, drove to the Texas 5, but a third-down reverse cost the Lions a yard and Alberto Vitiello kicked a 21-yard field goal with 10:38 left in the first half.

The stalemate survived until the final play of the second quarter when Valek kicked a 40-yard field goal to give the Longhorns a 6-3 lead.

Texas struck suddenly to go ahead. Penn State had moved to the Longhorn 40, but with 19 seconds remaining in the half Texas linebacker Glenn Gaspard made a one-handed interception of a Hufnagel

JOE
PATERNO
ERA

Franco Harris (34) bulls through the Texas line during the third quarter. Harris finished with 47 yards rushing.

Texas quarterback Eddie Phillips loses most of his jersey as he is dropped for a 6-yard loss by Jim Laslavic (47) of Penn State.

Texas' Dennis Ladd, right, lost control of the ball after a hard hit by Penn State's John Skorupan (81) in the second quarter. Texas went into halftime with a 6-3 advantage, but the second half turned ugly for the Longhorns, who yielded 27 points.

Coach Joe Paterno, left, leads the Nittany Lions in a victory cheer following Penn State's thrashing of Texas in the 1972 Cotton Bowl.

pass and returned it 23 yards to the 40.

Two of Phillips' passes to split end Pat Kelley set up Valek's second field goal. Coming into the game, he had missed five of six attempts.

Forcing Penn State to scramble after the ground-control attack of the wishbone offense, Texas controlled the ball for 16:59 of the first half, but twice lost scoring opportunities because of fumbles and ran for only 199 yards.

Defensive end Jim Laslavic, keying on Phillips much of the time, made 10 tackles in the first half.

Texas' third fumble proved costly. On the opening series of the second half, Phillips fumbled a handoff. Laslavic accidentally kicked in 10 yards downfield and Lions linebacker Charlie Zapiec outran Don Burrisk for the ball, covering it on the Longhorn 41.

It took Penn State just five plays to earn a 10-6 lead, only four minutes into the third quarter. Mitchell, who had 48 yards rushing on 11 carries in the first half, hit the middle for 20 and, a play later, Hufnagel drilled a pass to tight end Bob Parsons at the Texas 1. Mitchell bucked over for the touchdown and Vitiello converted.

Less than three minutes later, Penn State struck again. On the second play after a Texas punt, Hufnagel rolled to his right at the State 35 and threw a strike to split end Scott Sharzynski, who had gotten 15 yards behind Texas safetyman Mike Bayer. The 65-yard pass play gave Penn State a 17-6 lead with 8:44 to play in the third quarter.

Penn State 16 LSU 9

January 1, 1974 | Miami, Fla.

Paterno Proclaims 1973 Lions: 'Best Team I Ever Had'

JOE
PATERNO
ERA

By Bill Heufelder

The Pittsburgh Press

If Penn State is not the best college football team in the land, it is No. 1 among the eight clubs Joe Paterno has coached at the school. Who says so? Joe Paterno.

"This is the best team I've ever had," he said after the fifth–ranked Lions beat stubborn LSU, 16-9, tonight in the Orange Bowl on a surface that, if it were used as a bath mat, would cause more fatalities than automobiles.

Paterno conducted his own poll among the players in the dressing room. "The vote was unanimous," he grinned. "We're No. 1.

"Seriously, I don't know if we're No. 1, but we have as much right as anyone to be there. We're 12-0. I'm not going to say we're better than anyone else. That's silly. But we're as good as anyone else until someone beats us."

Well, LSU, twice-beaten during the regular season, had the best chance of any Penn State opponent this year. What the Tigers couldn't overcome was the Penn State defense and sturdy pass blocking that

Penn State	3	13	0	0 —	16
Louisiana State	7	0	2	0 —	9

enabled Tom Shuman to combine with Chuck Herd on a spectacular 72-yard scoring play.

Neither club could conquer the treacherous Poly-Turf, soaked by a pre-game shower.

" LSU was the quickest, toughest opponent against us for the longest stretch," Paterno complimented.

The officials perhaps buoyed LSU's persevering spirit with a couple of calls which, as the unerring television instant replay attested, proved they used bad judgment.

On Penn State's first series of the second quarter, Herd snapped up a long Shuman pass in full stride near the end line. An official ruled Herd had stepped out of the end zone before catching the ball. The camera

JOE
PATERNO
ERA

Penn State's Chuck Herd (25) is off and running — and behind the LSU secondary — on a 72-yard touchdown pass from Tom Shuman in the first half of the Nittany Lions' 16-9 Orange Bowl victory.

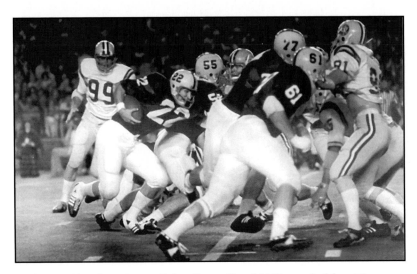

Penn State quarterback Tom Shuman (12) was only 6-for-17, but his TD pass to Chuck Herd was the game's key play.

Heisman Trophy winner John Cappelletti (22) was held to 50 yards, but scored once.

94

showed otherwise.

The Lions surrendered the ball on Brian Masella's punt, but held the Tigers inside the 20, forcing them to kick.

Gary Hayman, who led the nation in punt-return average, was well on his way to a touchdown runback when the play was called dead. An official signaled Hayman had touched a knee to the ground as he slipped on the Poly-Turf at the start of the run. Again, the replay proved the official wrong.

"I asked the referee on the next series and he said my knee touched and that was the only way I could have been ruled down," said Hayman, who had outraced the LSU defense at the 25 when an official motioned for him to stop.

"I didn't argue with him," Hayman said, "but I know my knee didn't touch."

The series ended successfully, however, when Herd came back to snatch Shuman's long pass with one hand and carry it into the end zone with two defenders in futile pursuit for a 72-yard scoring play.

Chris Bahr, who gave another zany kicking performance — hitting a 44-yard field goal yet missing an extra point — converted and sent the Lions ahead, 10-3. The soccer all-American connected on only 32 of 42 conversions during the regular season.

With 2:19 left in the half, John Cappelletti completed a 74-yard drive by hurtling over the stacked LSU defense from the 2.

A Heisman Trophy winner who had twice rushed for more than 1,000 yards in a season, the big tailback ran out of running room against the Tigers. Despite the absence of two regular linebackers, they held him to 50 yards in 26 carries, a meager 1.6 average.

"The holes weren't there," admitted his favorite blocker, guard Mark Markovich. "We just had trouble blocking their defenses."

Cappelletti, who suffered a slightly sprained ankle last Friday, refused to use the injury as an excuse. "No, it didn't bother me," he said. "Their defense just played well. Their linebackers were plugging the holes. I don't feel badly. I just tried to do the best I could."

Cappelletti was bothered by the Poly-Turf, calling it "the worst surface I ever played on."

Paterno said he thought "Cappy played a good game," despite netting only 50 yards. "The trouble was we weren't making the holes."

With 1:30 left in the half, LSU was in trouble with a fourth-and-one situation on its 19, so Penn State called a time out, hoping to conserve enough time to increase its 16-7 lead.

Instead, a Lions penalty on the LSU punt and the clever maneuvering of quarterback Mike Miley soon put the ball on the Penn State 9 with 11 seconds left.

Miley then hit Joe Fakier on a four-yard gain that demoralized LSU coach Charlie McClendon. "We thought he was gonna score," McClendon said, "but Fakier got stuck." Defensive back Jim Bradley rushed up to flatten the receiver.

"We didn't anticipate that," McClendon said. "That man (Bradley) was not supposed to be anywhere near Fakier, but he ignored our wide man."

Without any more time outs, the Tigers, trailing 16-7, could not make use of the final two seconds. Miley elected to throw the ball away in an unsuccessful effort to kill the clock.

Early in the fourth quarter, it was Randy Crowder, Penn State's all-American defensive tackle, who confused the line and picked off Miley's pass over the middle at the LSU 39.

"He started to go inside me," explained another all-American, stumpy guard Tyler Lafauci, "then he went outside and back inside again. Then he just stood there with his hands up in the air.

"I didn't know what to think."

The Tigers moved into a position to at least gain a tie when Masella fell on a high snap from center in the end zone for a safety.

So the Lions turned once more to their strength — the defense — to preserve the third Orange Bowl triumph of the Paterno era.

Making what proved to be their last serious threat, the Tigers, on fourth-and-three at the Penn State 27, called on their leading runner,

LSU coach Charlie McClendon, left and Penn State coach Joe Paterno shake hands after the Nittany Lions' victory.

Brad Davis. He took a pitchout, but quickly was upset by linebacker Doug Allen and went down at the 31, a four-yard loss.

"I called a switch at the line before the snap," Allen said, "so I took the 'pitch' man and the end in front of me covered the quarterback. The way they lined up dictated it."

Only once did the Tigers dominate the Penn State defensive unit and that was on the opening drive when they scored within four minutes.

"We weren't taking off," Crowder said. "Instead of making things happen, we were letting them make things happen. After that, we started taking off."

Linebacker Ed O'Neil took off on the subject of the polls and Notre Dame's 24-23 win over Alabama in the Sugar Bowl, which was billed as the national championship.

"I think we're the number one team in the country," he protested.

"I heard a lot of talk on TV last night about Notre Dame saying it's the champion. I don't think they won the championship because they haven't played us."

JOE
PATERNO
ERA

CAPPELLETTI: An Iron Horse Who Rumbled to the Heisman Trophy

By Steve Halvonik

Pittsburgh Post-Gazette

John Cappelletti hadn't planned on talking about his 11-year-old brother Joey, who was stricken with leukemia, when he stood to deliver his 1973 Heisman Trophy acceptance speech.

Most of the things I had put on paper were the mundane things — people to thank, football memories," Cappelletti said."I had been thinking about Joseph, some things had been going through my head. When I saw my family sitting down front, something just clicked."

Cappelletti, who was seated next to Vice President Gerald Ford at the dais, opened his speech with the usual tributes to teammates, parents, and other acquaintances. But his voice began to quake as he focused on Joey and his brother's losing fight with cancer.

Most of the guests at The Waldorf-Astoria were unaware of Joey's illness. Many began to weep after John recalled the day that Penn State coach Joe Paterno had visited his house on a recruiting trip and found Joey on the couch, ill.

"A lot of people think I go through a lot on Saturdays, getting bumps and bruises," John Cappelletti said, holding back tears."But for me, it's only on Saturdays and only in the fall. For Joey, it's all year round and it's a never-ending battle.

"The Heisman Trophy is more his than mine because he's been a great inspiration to me ... if I can dedicate this trophy to him tonight and give him a couple of days of happiness, it would mean everything."

By now,"everybody in the room was fighting runaway emotion," Paterno said in his autobiography, *Paterno: By the Book*. "The vice president sat there all flushed. His eyes, I thought, glistened."

Even Bishop Fulton J. Sheen, a polished speaker who had to deliver the benediction, found Cappelletti a tough act to follow.

"Maybe for the first time in your lives you have heard a speech from the heart and not from the lips," Sheen told the audience."Part of John's triumph was made by Joseph's sorrow. You don't need a blessing.

JOE
PATERNO
ERA

God has already blessed you in John Cappelletti."

Cappelletti's powerful speech resonated across the nation, striking a deep emotional chord in football and non-football fans alike. It inspired a made-for-TV movie, called *Something For Joey*. And it has become part of Heisman history.

"John's acceptance speech is considered the most moving ever given at these ceremonies," The Downtown Athletic Club, the Heisman's sponsor, says in its annual awards program.

Joseph Cappelletti lost his fight with leukemia, passing away in 1976. But his memory still shines brightly in John's home in Laguna Niguel, Calif.

The Heisman Trophy that he dedicated to his brother sits on a mantel in the family room. Pictures of Joseph, clutching the Heisman, are on display in the children's playroom.

Cappellitti says he still thinks about his brother, whom he always calls "Joseph," whenever he looks at the Heisman.

"I still have vivid memories of the awards dinner and my family," he says.

And of his unprecedented career at Penn State.

Cappelletti is the only Nittany Lion to win a Heisman Trophy, and it came at the end of what still ranks as the second-best rushing season in school history. Cappelletti plowed for 1,522 yards and 17 touchdowns and led Penn State to its third undefeated season in six years.

Only Lydell Mitchell has ever gained more yards in a season, picking up 1,567 in 1971.

Cappelletti's 286 rushing attempts and three 200-yard rushing games still stand as school records.

Although he started at tailback for only two seasons, Cappelletti still ranks sixth in career rushing, with 2,639 yards.

The converted defensive back rushed for 100 or more yards 13 times in his storybook career with the Lions, averaging 5.1 yards a carry.

In a scene from the CBS-TV movie, "Something for Joey," John Cappelletti (Mark Singer) listens to advice from his coach, Joe Paterno (Paul Piscerni).

JOE PATERNO ERA

Cappelletti rushed for 1,117 yards as a junior, but wasn't mentioned as a leading Heisman contender before his senior season. He sat out Penn State's 14-0 loss to Oklahoma at the end of his junior year, denying him valuable exposure in the national media.

Cappelletti picked up 735 yards during Penn State's 7-0 start in 1973, but remained little more than a darkhorse because of the media bias against Eastern football.

Cappelletti forced everyone to take a second look at himself and at Penn State with an incredible closing kick — 787 rushing yards in the final four games.

Cappelletti still recalls how it all started, with a private pep talk from Paterno just before Game 8, against Maryland.

Paterno told Cappelletti not to worry about Heisman speculation. Focus instead on what you can can control — your performance on the field, Paterno counseled. The rest will fall into place.

Cappelletti went out and carried the ball a school-record 37 times, for 202 yards, against the Terrapins.

"That was the game that started the boom for Cappelletti as a Heisman candidate," Paterno recalled.

Cappelletti followed that with 41 carries for 220 yards in a 35-29

John Cappelletti brushes a tear from his eye as he returns to his seat following an emotion-filled speech in which he dedicated his Heisman Trophy to his younger brother, Joseph, who was battling cancer.

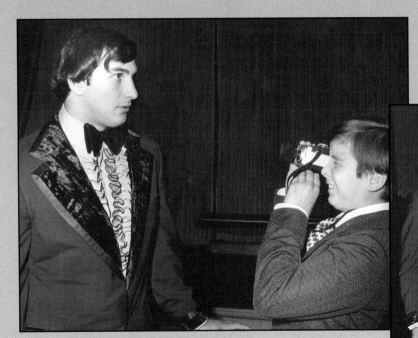

Prior to the Heisman Dinner, Cappelletti poses for a photo being taken by his younger brother, Joseph.

victory over North Carolina State.

"I think I probably got as much, or more, satisfaction out of that game than from any other at Penn State," he says.

Cappelletti continued his roll by bulling for 204 yards against Ohio University, giving him an NCAA-record three straight games of 200 or more yards rushing.

By the season finale, Cappelletti was in the thick of the Heisman race. He clinched the trophy with his 161-yard effort in a 35-13 win over the Pitt Panthers, sealing Penn State's undefeated (11-0) regular season.

Penn State's Orange Bowl matchup against LSU was anti-climactic.

In spite of their undefeated record, the Lions were a non-factor in the championship picture. The glamour game was Notre Dame and Alabama in the Sugar Bowl.

Penn State beat LSU, 16-9, but finished fifth in the final Associated Press and UPI polls.

Notre Dame, which upset Alabama, 24-23, was crowned No. 1 by The Associated Press.

Paterno was livid that his Lions had been snubbed yet again. So he conducted his own poll in the Penn State locker room. He came out and proclaimed Penn State No. 1, and ordered championship rings for players and coaches.

Paterno's gesture notwithstanding, the Orange Bowl remained a letdown for players, Cappelletti admits.

"I think the bowl game was kind of overshadowed because we couldn't win the national championship," says Cappy, who gained just 50 yards on 26 carries against LSU.

100

Cappelletti spent 10 years in the National Football League, but never reached the heights he attained at Penn State.

The Los Angeles Rams took him on the first round of the 1974 draft, but he languished on the bench for two season before moving into the starting lineup.

He gained 2,246 yards in six seasons with the Rams, including 688 in 1976.

He sat out 1979 on injured reserve and the Rams dealt him the following year to the San Diego Chargers. He played there four years and retired after the 1983 season.

He was elected to the College Football Hall of Fame in 1993.

In this series of photos, Cappelletti shows the great talent that earned him both the Heisman and Maxwell trophies in 1973.

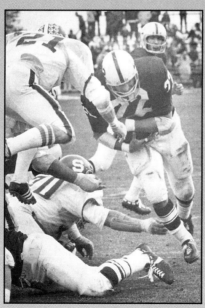 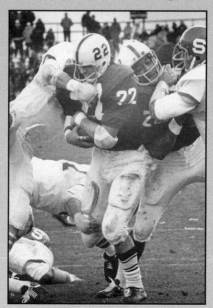 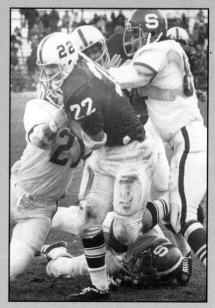

JOE PATERNO ERA

Penn State 41 Baylor 20

January 1, 1975 | Dallas, Tex.

Lions Turn Cinderella Bears into Pumpkins in Cotton Bowl

Penn State bloodied Cinderella's nose yesterday with its 41-20 victory over Baylor in the 39th annual Cotton Bowl.

The Bears, who rebounded dramatically from a 2-9 season to break Texas' six-year domination of the Southwest Conference, held together through the first half and emerged with a 7-3 lead.

They fell behind on the opening Penn State series of the third quarter when fullback Tom Donchez powered into the end zone from the 2, ending an 80-yard drive.

When Tom Shuman ignored Dennis DeLoach's fierce rush and lofted a perfectly thrown 49-yard scoring pass to freshman Jimmy Cefalo, Baylor turned into a pumpkin.

Shuman, who had passed erratically in the first half and once overlooked a receiver wide open at the Baylor 5, finished with 226 yards passing and the game's most valuable offensive player award.

| Penn State | 0 | 3 | 14 | 24 | — | 41 |
| Baylor | 7 | 0 | 7 | 6 | — | 20 |

The sixth-ranked Lions scored five successive times, beginning with Shuman's throw that pushed them ahead, 17-14, as they recovered from a bewildering retreat on the previous possession.

They incurred a double penalty on a play in which Donchez carried a swing pass 64 yards into the Baylor end zone. Teammate Jim Eaise was called for offensive pass interference and Shuman was slapped with a non-contact personal foul for flipping the official's flag.

"I apologized to the official," Shuman explained. "He told me, 'You're a pain in the —.' He was kind of sour all day."

Instead of a touchdown, the Lions were stuck on their own 12, from where Brian Masella punted.

"That wasn't a penalty," Coach Joe Paterno said. "That was a forfeit."

Penn State's Jimmy Cefalo (44) eludes the Baylor defense for a fourth-quarter touchdown. The Nittany Lions scored 24 points in the final period to turn a close game into a 41-20 rout.

Baylor fullback Pat McNeil is wrestled down by Penn State's Greg Murphy (82) and Rich Kriston (92).

JOE PATERNO ERA

The controversial play proved to be more costly to the Bears, who lost safety Ken Queensberry when a downfield block crumpled his right knee. Queensberry, although unable to return, received the game's defensive award for his 12 tackles and two fumble recoveries.

His absence seemed to allow more light into the Baylor pass defense, which already was relying on a pair of freshman cornerbacks.

"The passes and reverses," Baylor linebacker Derrel Luce said, "really started hurting us. We were always one play behind. On defense, you've got to control the tempo."

Yeah, like the Penn State defense. It stumbled into three offside penalties on the Bears' scoring drive in the first quarter, but owned the Bears in the second half.

Stubby Steve Beaird, a 1,000-yard rusher during the year, was held to 12 yards after gaining 72 in the opening half, as the Lions poured through Baylor to disrupt Neal Jeffrey's passing game.

"They did a super job of adjusting," said Jeffrey after managing seven of 19 completions and a tipped 35-yard touchdown pass that fell conveniently into the hands of Ricky Thompson in the third quarter.

"We should have given Neal more time on those passes," his center, Aubrey Schulz, said. "A bunch of times, Penn State stunted and that messed up our timing."

The tacklers arrived in bunches to bring down the 5-foot-6, 196-pound Beaird. "It wasn't the first hit that bother me," he said. "It was the second, third and fourth guys coming in."

After Cefalo's scoring catch, the Lions reverted to the power-I, with Donchez, who led all rushers with 116 yards, blocking for Neil Hutton, a darting, elusive sophomore.

Picking up 79 yards in 12 carriers, Hutton spurred Penn State to a touchdown, which came on Cefalo's three-yard run, and a 33-yard field goal by Chris Bahr midway through the final quarter that put Penn State in front, 27-14.

Baylor coach Grant Teaff, a Baptist deacon, said he was keeping the faith until safety Mike Johnson picked off Jeffrey's pass on first down and returned it to the Bears' 18. Five plays later, Shuman scored from the Bears' 2.

In the waning seconds, Joe Jackson, a reserve linebacker, offset a Baylor touchdown by returning an onside kick 50 yards for the final touchdown.

If Beaird was overwhelmed by the Penn State defense, he was short on his opinion of the Lions as a team.

"If Penn State played in the Southwest Conference," he said, "it would be hard for them to win it. They'd probably be in the top three, though."

It was an assessment that sounded like a fairy tale.

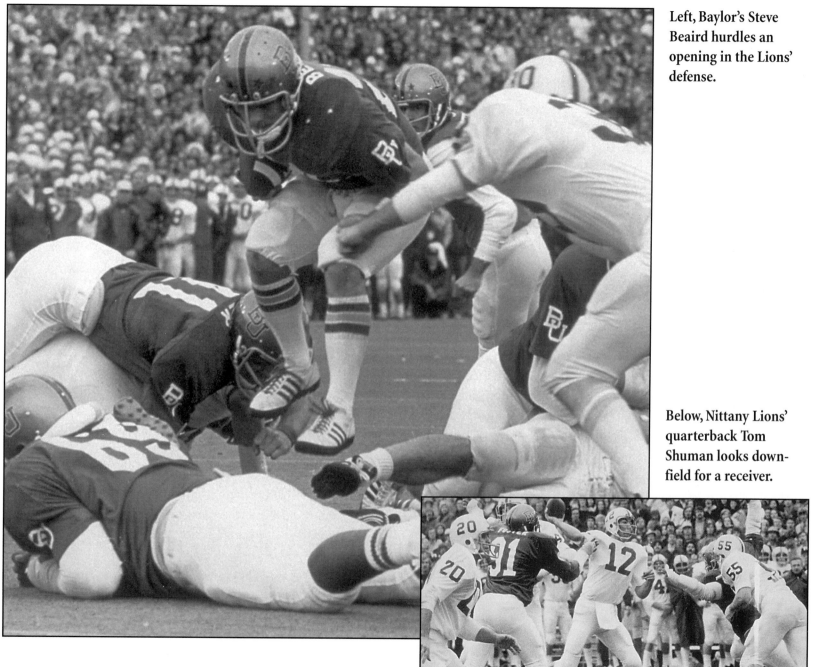

Left, Baylor's Steve Beaird hurdles an opening in the Lions' defense.

Below, Nittany Lions' quarterback Tom Shuman looks downfield for a receiver.

JOE PATERNO ERA

Penn State 7 Pittsburgh 6

November 22, 1975 | Pittsburgh, Pa.

Penn State Wins 'Kicking Game' Against Panthers

By Russ Franke

The Pittsburgh Press

For Carson Long, in his own tearful words, it was a "horrible thing" for him and the Pitt football team. For Penn State it was a beautiful thing. A 7-6 win in the clutch.

Penn State survived its toughest battle with Pitt in 10 years today, and a near-capacity crowd at Three Rivers Stadium and a national television audience saw a thriller that wound up as one of the most heartbreaking losses in Pitt history.

This was the year, Pitt people felt, to break Penn State's Eastern superiority, and the Panthers almost pulled it off with a brilliant defensive effort, only to miss their opportunities in a frenzied ending.

Long went into the game as one of the most accurate placement-kickers in the country as well as one of the proudest fathers — his wife, Peggy, had given birth to a baby girl only hours before — but the highly-keyed junior came out the most disappointed man in the world, missing field goals from the 13- and 35-yard lines in the final minute-and-a-half, plus a 51-yarder earlier in the fourth quarter.

Penn State	0	0	0	7 —	7
Pittsburgh	0	6	0	0 —	6

Pitt had scored first on Elliott Walker's 37-yard blast up the middle in the second period, but Tom Odell blocked Long's extra-point try, and it turned out to be the difference on the scoreboard.

The Nittany Lions got that one back on another big run, a naked 28-yard slash off left tackle in the middle of the final quarter. Chris Bahr's placement made it 7-6 and it was the third straight year Penn State was forced to come from behind late to beat the Panthers.

The win gave Penn State a 9-2 record to take into the Sugar Bowl against Alabama and the loss left Pitt at 7-4, the same record as last year, with a Dec. 26 date against Kansas in the Sun Bowl.

"Offensively, we got whipped up front," said Pitt's Johnny Majors, "But I've never seen a line play as well defensively as ours did. And I've never seen two

Pitt kicker Carson Long, right, missed three fourth-quarter field goals in the Panthers' 7-6 loss.

Chris Bahr's fourth-quarter extra point proved to be the difference in Penn State's victory.

teams hit that hard, especially on defense. My hat's off to Penn State for the way they played us."

Big hits by Al Romano, Don Parrish, Randy Cozens, Randy Holloway, Arnie Weatherington and Tom Perko, in particular, drew repeated roars from the Pitt fans in the chilled crowd of 46,846 (there were roughly 5,000 no-shows), as Pitt gained the edge defensively.

The Panthers knocked five fumbles loose and recovered three of them. They also picked an interception off Chuck Fusina, the freshman quarterback who relieved John Andress in the third period.

Joe Paterno had said beforehand there was no way his defense could stop Tony Dorsett, and Dorsett bolstered his bid for another all-American year by ripping off 125 yards on 28 carries, ending the regular season with 1,544 yards and a three-year total of 4,234.

"Overall, I thought we beat them in everything but the game," said Dorsett. "Football is funny — you play so good and you still wind up on the wrong end. I know how Carson Long feels. Remember, I fumbled on the 1-yard line at Notre Dame last year and we lost the game.

"Penn State did a good job on our option plays. They strung it out almost as good as West Virginia did. But that wasn't the reason we lost."

The Panthers indicated what kind of a tense struggle it would be when they gambled on their first series and won, with Matt Cavanaugh diving off the right corner for three yards and a first down at his 45. Apparently, they mustered their nerve to do it after Dorsett had breezed for 30 yards on his first carry of the game.

From then until the Panthers scored, however, it was purely a defensive struggle spiced by some mistakes on both sides, as State continued to play the option well and the Pitt defense kept the middle stopped against the running of Woody Petchel, Duane Taylor and Jimmy Cefalo, who played at tailback instead of wingback in a surprise switch by Paterno.

A couple of penalties for clipping and holding plus an interception by linebacker Ron Hostetler stopped the Panthers in the second quarter, and then it was Pitt's turn to create a turnover. Andress passed 20 yards to Mickey Shuler but Dennis Moorehead banged Shuler immediately to knock the ball away and recover on the State 48.

Dorsett hit a hole for 11 yards and then Walker broke into the middle, got some room with a fake and broke Gary Petercuskie's tackle on the way to a touchdown.

The Lions got a break when Larry Swider went back to punt at his 26 and Ron Coder blitzed in cleanly to tackle him, but Pitt got the ball back when Randy Cozens belted Petchel and the ball squirted away, Randy Holloway recovering.

Late in the third period, Fusina threw deep for Tom Donovan and Bob Jury made an easy interception at his 11.

Fusina, thrilled to be home for the first time in three months — he is the latest in a long line of quarterbacks from McKees Rocks — said he was aware that other receivers were open but that "I was going for all the marbles. I guess I messed up."

The Lions forced another punt to the State 29, and this time the Lions finally got their offense together to march back all the way.

Pitt coach Johnny Majors and Paterno visit prior to the game.

JOE PATERNO ERA

A pass interference call put the ball on the 42 and Cefalo, Fusina and Steve Geise took turns carrying to the Pitt 28. Geise was supposed to hit inside, looking for a first down against a short yardage defense, but the hole wasn't there and he veered left, catching the Pitt cornerback inside, and scored untouched.

Here the going got even stickier. The Panthers gang-tackled Fusina at the sideline, and when he fumbled, Jury came up with it on the State 29 with 3:49 to play and Pitt appeared headed for a sure win. Cavanaugh ducked a fierce rush and threw a 28-yarder to Gordon Jones who made a spectacular catch on the 6.

Mike Johnson made a great touchdown-saving tackle on the sideline.

Pitt was in business, but so was the State defense. Walker was stopped at the State 1 and Dorsett lost to the 9. Walker got 3 yards in moving the ball toward the center of the field for Long, but his try for a 23-yarder sailed wide right and it appeared Pitt was done.

But the Pitt defense came up with another giant effort and forced Bahr to punt to the Pitt 40. There were 37 seconds left, and the Panthers got yet another chance when Cavanaugh found Rodney Clark open and threw. The Lions were called for interference at their 35 and then Cavanaugh passed to Karl Farmer on the 25, Farmer hopping out of bounds to stop the clock with nine seconds left.

Long's field goal try of 45 yards dropped in front of the goal post and Penn State had its 10th straight win over Pitt.

Long, comforted in the arms of his sidekick and placement-holder Swider, was choked with disappointment as he left Three Rivers. Did the blocked extra-point affect his concentration on his field goal attempts?

"What a horrible thing," he said. "I had everything lined up. The snaps were good and the holds were good. There was no excuse for it."

Penn State 7 Alabama 14

Alabama Defeats No. 1 Lions in Dramatic Goal-Line Stand

JOE PATERNO ERA

By Russ Franke

The Pittsburgh Press

For Penn State, the moment of truth was 92 years and six inches away.

That moment came deep into Alabama territory and deep into the fourth quarter of today's Sugar Bowl show-down between No. 1 Penn State and No. 2 Alabama, and it went deep into the brain of the man making the most decisive defensive play of the collegiate football season — Barry Krause, an Alabama linebacker who underlined his all-America stamp by stopping Mike Guman on the six-inch line on fourth and goal.

And the Crimson Tide went on to win the game, 14-7, and the national title.

"It was one of the hardest hits I ever made," said Krause, and it deprived Penn State of a prime chance to win the first national championship in 92 years of football. The hit left Krause even more stunned than the Penn State offense, and he lay flat on the ground long enough for the trainers to come onto the Superdome turf and treat him.

Penn State	0	0	7	0 —	7
Alabama	0	7	7	0 —	14

"I wasn't really unconscious but I was dazed," said Krause. "I busted my helmet. From watching films, we knew they scored a lot of touchdowns by diving over the top, and I knew in my heart I had to be there to stop him."

The play typified an afternoon of superior defense by both teams, and for once Penn State's defense, the best in the country going in, came out second best. The Nittany Lions gained a great deal of notoriety by limiting their regular-season opponents to 54 yards a game, but Alabama exceeded that by holding Penn State to 19 yards rushing, and that is another story in itself.

Krause and his coach, Paul (Bear) Bryant, said that Alabama's pass rush was the big factor, something the Tide worked on especially hard

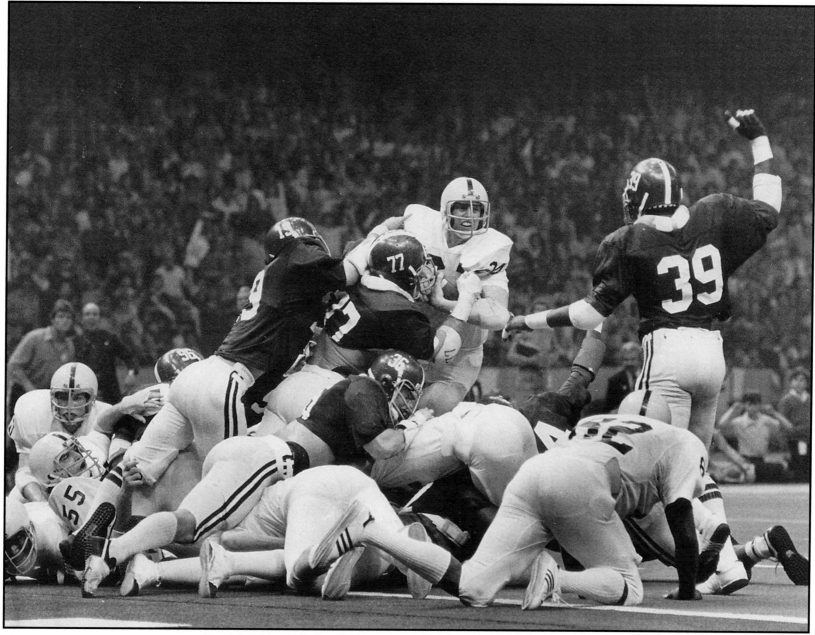

JOE
PATERNO
ERA

Alabama's defense stops Lions halfback Mike Guman in a memorable fourth-quarter, goal-line stand.

Alabama halfback Major Ogilvie (42) rips through the Lions defense for 4 yards.

Jim Bob Harris (9) steals a pass intended for Lions receiver Bob Bassett.

112

in order to take away Chuck Fusina's passing game. Fusina was caught seven times for minus 64 yards, accounting for the low team rushing total.

"I don't believe I've ever been associated with a team that did so well on defense," said Bryant. "I think we could have beaten any team in America today, and today is what counted, wasn't it? We went into the game trying to play as if we were two points behind all the time."

Alabama never was behind, actually. A last minute pass just before halftime gave the Tide a touchdown lead. Penn State tied the score in the third quarter and Alabama got the winning touchdown four minutes later following Lou Ikner's 62-yard punt return — an event that seldom occurs against Penn State — to the 11-yard line.

Four plays later, Major Ogilvie became at least a general by taking Jeff Rutledge's cleverly delayed pitchout eight yards off the left side, and there was nothing Pete Harris or Rick Milot could do about the execution of the play, the kind of wishbone play that makes Alabama a perennial power.

There was no question that the wishbone was the toughest option offense Penn State had to battle all season, perhaps for a number of seasons. The Tide rolled for 208 yards out of it, with halfback Tony Nathan getting 127. Even so, it required supreme efforts, particularly by Lance Mehl, Bruce Clark and Matt Millen, to prevent the Tide from dominating the game.

On a Tide touchdown pass just before the halftime, the effectiveness of a well-manned wishbone asserted itself. The irony in that a guard-oriented offense lends itself to the long bomb, and that is also another story that revealed itself after the game when Rutledge talked to the reporters.

"That touchdown pass was a new play," said Rutledge. "The man I threw it to was actually the decoy, Bruce Bolton. He was the third man and I went to him when I realized he had his man one-on-one (sophomore Karl McCoy). They had our fullback and tight end in a crowd."

The pass was for 30 yards and it ended an 80-yard drive that started with 1:11 to go before halftime.

Until then, defense was the name of the game and even though Alabama controlled the ball and kept State out of field position with the punting of Woody Umphrey, it could be said that the Nittany Lions defense was better in the clutch simply because most of the first half was played in Lions territory.

Penn State didn't make real penetration until the TD drive that started with six minutes remaining in the third period. Harris, known as "Franco's brother," but now a celebrity in his own right as the leading interceptor in the nation, picked off a Rutledge pass at the Alabama 48.

The Lions quickly capitalized, living up to their tradition for the only time in the game. Fusina hit Guman with a 25-yard sideline pass to the

Scott Fitzkee scored Penn State's only touchdown with this end-zone catch.

Tide 19, and after Guman picked up two yards, Fusina showed the Superdome crowd of 76,824 his arm by drilling the ball deep into the end zone.

Scott Fitzkee also showed the crowd on the national TV audience something — a great deal of hands and feet. He made a Lynn Swann-type catch over the head of the defender and somehow kept his feet inside the end line for a TD. Matt Bahr, itching on the sidelines all afternoon, got his only chance to kick a ball through the upright and it was 7-7.

Mehl, Millen, Larry Kubin and Joe Lally pulled the wishbone apart in the next series to force a punt. But State couldn't move the sticks and when Fitzkee had to punt, Ikner took the ball down the left sidelines and made a nice cut inside his blocking for 62 yards.

Freshman Matt Bradley saved a touchdown by dragging down Ikner from behind, but it served only to delay the Tide's winning thrust on Ogilvie's eight-yard run.

113

Penn State 31 Ohio State 19

Penn State Grounds Buckeyes' Air Attack in Fiesta Bowl

JOE
PATERNO
ERA

By Bob Black

The Pittsburgh Press

Penn State coach Joe Paterno called it "simply a matter of making a minor adjustment in the second half."

Of course, the result was very much like trading in a .22 and replacing it with a cannon. Or replacing a school of guppies in your fish tank with a school of piranha.

That's basically what happened in front of a record-breaking Fiesta Bowl crowd of 66,738 fans here yesterday at Sun Devil Stadium.

And that "minor adjustment" Paterno talked about resulted in Penn State turning around a nine-point halftime deficit which had seen Ohio State quarterback Art Schlichter passing for 244 yards into a complete shutout in the third quarter.

That's right. No yards passing. No yards running. Nothing.

And it also resulted in the Lions turning this into a 10-win season via a 31-19 victory over Ohio State which could push Penn State as high as fifth or sixth in the final ratings after all the bowl games have been played.

Penn State	7	3	6	15	— 31
Ohio State	6	13	0	0	— 19

It also occurred after Penn State safety Pete Harris had been removed from the game when he suffered stretched ligaments in his leg at the end of the first half.

That resulted in replacing Harris, who is Penn State's most experienced defensive back as a fifth-year senior and who also stands 6-2, with 5-8 sophomore Dan Biondi from Penn Hills.

Considering that Biondi's only previous games with significant playing time were in easy wins over Colgate, Texas A&M and Temple, any betting man would have wagered the house, the car and most of his negotiable paper that Schlichter would continue picking apart the Lions' secondary in the second half.

It didn't work that way, however.

JOE
PATERNO
ERA

Curt Warner, (25) outsprints Ohio State's Ray Ellis (27) and Vince Skillings (48) on a 63-yard touchdown run.

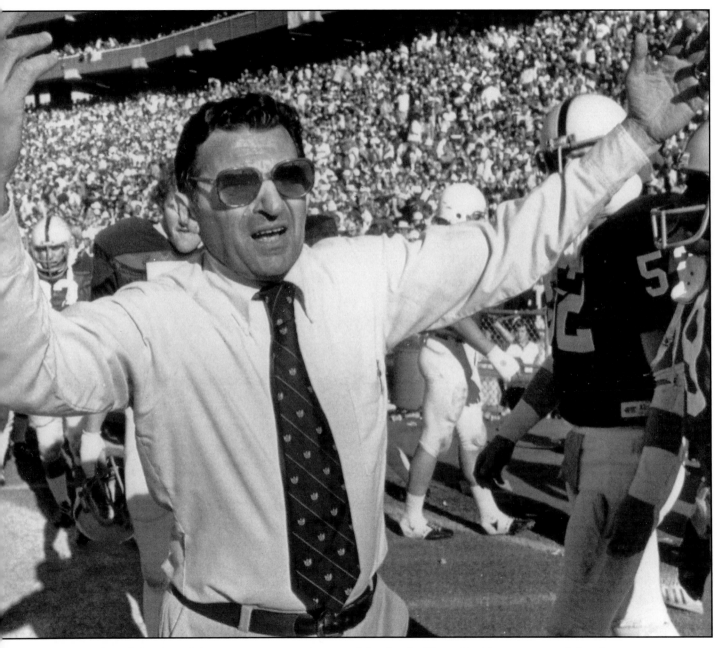

With Biondi subbing for Harris and the Lions defensive line taking control of Ohio State's offensive line, Penn State was able to keep the Buckeye seniors 0-for-career in four bowl appearances.

And to say that it was a significant win was like saying the Mona Lisa is a significant work of art.

"Beating a team like Ohio State on national TV helps restore our reputation," said senior defensive tackle Frank Case, who was named the defensive player of the game. "Against Pitt we thought we outplayed them, yet we lost — on national TV."

"And against Nebraska we turned the ball over seven times and lost — on national TV."

"So this time we were able to win one of those BIG football games."

And a big reason for that was the usual strong defensive performance turned in by the Lions in the second half while the offense was taking its cue from the defense and playing ball control.

116   **After defeating Ohio State, 31-19, Joe Paterno joins in the Fiesta Bowl postgame celebration.**

"There's no question one group helps out the other," said Penn State offensive guard Sean Farrell, who along with seniors Bill Dugan and Bob Jagers was a principal reason the Lions were able to rush for 351 yards and pass for 117 more against the Buckeyes.

"We use a lot of people when we play. As a result, our starters are still fresh late in the game. It think that was a key. They (Ohio State) seemed to be tiring late in that game."

They probably were tired of chasing Curt Warner, who finished with the most productive rushing performance of his career — 155 yards on 18 carries — fullback Booker Moore and backup tailbacks Joel Coles and Jon Williams and backup fullback Mike Meade.

"You gotta be impressed with their running game," said Penn State coach Earle Bruce. "They keep bringing in new backs. And they keep picking up yardage with them."

But in the first half, it was Ohio State with Schlichter passing to Doug Donley and Gary Williams which rolled up the impressive stats.

After Warner gave Penn State its only significant offensive play of the first half — going 64 yards for a touchdown on the Lions' first play from scrimmage of the game — it was left to Dr. Schlichter to operate on the Penn State secondary.

First he hit Donley with a 23-yard touchdown pass to complete an 83-yard, six-play drive accomplished in less than two minutes.

When Buckeye kicker Vlade Janakievski missed his first extra point of the year after hitting 45 straight, the Lions still held a one-point margin.

But again Schlichter went to work, this time covering 84 yards in seven plays in less than three minutes. He gave the Buckeyes the lead on a 32-yard touchdown pass to Williams.

This time Case dropped Schlichter in his own backfield on the Buckeyes' attempt at the two point conversion.

Again Schlichter chipped away at the Lions secondary and covered 77 yards in seven plays and just one minute 35 seconds, and Penn State looked like easy pickings.

But after Herb Menhardt closed out the first-half scoring with with a 38-yard field goal, Penn State put on a new game face for the second half.

"Our defense was being hurt by their inside curl pattern," said Paterno. "And they were completing a lot of short passes over the middle. So we decided we'd have to adjust a few things and take those plays away from them."

One thing Paterno might not have been figuring having to adjust, however, was replacing Harris with Biondi at safety. But Biondi, who has been primarily a special teams player this season, was ready.

"I wasn't concerned about them throwing over me," Biondi said of the prospect of Schlichter attempting to hit Donley and Williams against him.

"Their receivers aren't any bigger than ours. And I go against ours in practice. Besides that, Coach Paterno had us all ready to go this week." Because of the heat we knew a lot of people would be playing in this game."

And in the second half, those people combined to wear down an Ohio State team which never was able to regain its first-half form.

"They started stunting and playing more man-to-man coverage," Schlichter said of Penn State's second-half performance. "Our game plan was to throw on them. But we didn't have the field advantage in the second half we did in the first."

The Lions started their second-half comeback by covering 75 yards in 10 plays with quarterback Todd Blackledge bootlegging the final 4 yards for the touchdown.

Then, in the fourth quarter, the Lions took advantage of good field position set up by a 17-yard punt return by Williams.

The freshman big-play tailback, who runs behind Warner and Coles at that position, scored the go-ahead touchdown by plunging four yards for the score.

And Moore finished off the Buckeyes by scoring on a 37-yard run in the final minute of play.

JOE PATERNO ERA

Penn State 48 Pittsburgh 14

November 28, 1981 | Pittsburgh, Pa.

Lions Ground Marino, Pierce Pitt's No. 1 Dream

JOE PATERNO ERA

By Bob Smizik

The Pittsburgh Press

Penn State	0	14	17	17 —	48
Pittsburgh	14	0	0	0 —	14

No one ever said that this was a football team that could not be beaten. But no one ever dreamt, not even Joe Paterno, that this was a football team that could be beaten so badly.

No more national championship talk, no more No. 1 rating. The talking is over, the football playing is over. Penn State is a winner. Is it ever!

Fumbles, interceptions and penalties were a part of this monumental defeat of the Pitt Panthers, but more than those critical errors it was a great football team that did them in yesterday.

Penn State spotted Pitt two early touchdowns, thus allowing the Panthers to believe they were some kind of invincible juggernaut, then went to work, putting six touchdowns and two field goals on the scoreboard while the No. 3 scoring offense in the country didn't get another point as the Lions roared to a 48-14 win before 60,260.

The No. 1-ranked and Sugar Bowl-bound Panthers (10-1) will prob-

ably fall to the bottom half of the Top 10. The ninth-ranked and Fiesta Bowl-bound Lions (9-2), who destroyed the No. 1 defense in the nation, should move up several notches.

"I never dreamt this could happen," said Pitt tight end John Brown. "When it rains, it pours. And it really rained on us today."

It rained in all kinds of forms on the Panthers, who had not lost at home since losing to Penn State in the final game of the 1977 season.

Much-maligned Penn State quarterback Todd Blackledge threw for 262 yards and two touchdowns. Forgotten Kenny Jackson, who had caught only 14 passes all season, made the Pitt secondary look like amateurs, grabbing five balls for 158 yards and two touchdowns. Injured Curt Warner was healthy enough to rush for 104 yards on 21 carries and

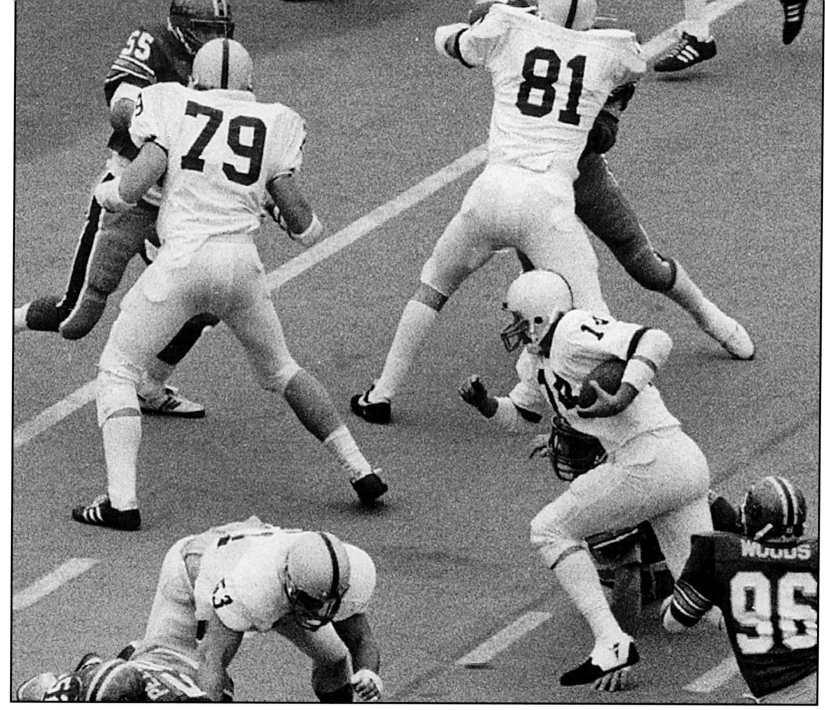

Penn State quarterback Todd Blackledge (14) tied the game on an 8-yard run in the second quarter.

Pitt's Michael Woods (96) applies a bear hug to Lions quarterback Todd Blackledge.

became the fourth Penn State back in history to go over 1,000 yards for the season.

From Warner, such an afternoon is not unexpected. But from Blackledge and Jackson, such games have been rare this season.

"We didn't play that well in the secondary," said Pitt coach Jackie Sherrill.

Free safety Tom Flynn was more colorful. "He (Jackson) is good, no doubt about that," said Flynn. "We didn't expect that at all. We didn't really know how good he was. He was having a bad year, but he turned around and put it in our face."

It didn't start that way, not that way at all. A Pitt Stadium crowd which was some 4,000 beyond capacity because of special bleachers in the end zone, figured it was in on a rout right from the start, but that it would be the Panthers doing the routing.

Pitt quarterback Dan Marino was positively brilliant, completing nine of 10 passes in the first quarter as the Panthers scored on their first two possessions.

But if Pitt fans and players were expecting a rout, Paterno was not. "Nobody can stay that hot all day," said Paterno.

And sure enough, Marino was intercepted in the end zone on the first play of the second quarter. It was the first in a series of interceptions (four), fumbles lost (three) and penalties (13) that, along with a fine Penn State defense, were to render the heretofore explosive Pitt offensive null and void.

But for the first 11 minutes of the game, the Panthers were near-perfect on both offense and defense. While scoring 14 points and not having to punt, the Panthers also held the Lions to minus yardage.

The Panthers moved 48 yards for their first score, with Marino passing 28 yards to Dwight Collins, who had a superb day with six catches, for the touchdown.

And that was it. For a while, the Panthers continued to move the ball, but as the mistakes mounted to sap their motivation, and as Penn State started to score and score and score, Pitt became a shell of the team that had won 17 straight games.

Starting on the 20, following Roger Jackson's interception, the Lions began their incredible comeback. With Blackledge completing short passes and with Pitt defensive end Al Wenglikowski contributing a 15-yard, face-mask penalty, the Lions moved to the Pitt 30, where Flynn — on a safety blitz — was a millisecond from nailing him, Blackledge passed 28 yards to tight end Mike McCloskey. Mike Meade scored on the next play and the Lions were in business.

Later in the quarter, with the Lions in possession on their own 39, Jackson was in a footrace down the middle of the field with Flynn and Pappy Thomas, who were matching him stride for stride. But when Blackledge put the ball in the air, Jackson turned on the afterburners and all Flynn and Thomas could do was hope he would drop the ball.

He didn't. Flynn made the tackle on the 8. Blackledge then scored on the next play.

Pitt had a chance to recapture the momentum before the half when Pat McQuaide recovered Jackson's fumble on a punt on the Penn State 41. Marino passed 19 yards to sophomore Bill Wallace, and Bryan Thomas, who became the third Pitt runner in history to pass 1,000 yards, ran for 6 to move the ball to the 22.

A Marino to Thomas pass put the ball on the 4, but the play was called back when offensive guard Rob Fada was called for a personal foul on Penn State defensive end Walker Lee Ashley.

"He was talking trash and throwing cheap shots all afternoon," said Fada. "On that play he hit me in the jaw. The ref had to see it. But they had lost control of the game. But I shouldn't have done it. I lost my cool."

And Pitt lost a probable touchdown. On the next play, Wayne DiBartola fumbled.

Pitt continued to make mistakes in the second half. On the fourth play of the half, sophomore fullback Bill Beach, playing in place of DiBartola, who had injured his ankle, fumbled after running for 13 yards to the Penn State 44. That was all Jackson and Blackledge needed.

From the Pitt 42, Blackledge hit Jackson almost perfectly a step from the sideline at the 10. But instead of going out of bounds, Jackson pivoted back to the middle of the field, leaving Flynn and strong safety Dan Short in the lurch as he ran for a touchdown.

A few minutes later Jackson left cornerback Tim Lewis some 15 yards behind him as he took a 45-yard pass for a touchdown.

JOE PATERNO ERA

Penn State's Roger Jackson hammers Pitt receiver Julius Dawkins (80), sending the ball into the air for the Nittany Lions' Mark Robinson to grab an interception.

"Poor Tim Lewis," said Pitt defensive coordinator Foge Fazio. "He guessed wrong and got burned."

And the fire was out of the Panthers.

Other than a 32-yard pass to Collins, which was followed by three plays that netted minus-6 yards, the Panthers had no more offense in the third quarter.

And still Penn State came. Pitt was down and the Lions wanted lots more. And they got lots more.

Brian Franco added field goals of 39 and 38 yards to start the fourth quarter and those were followed by a sustained drive which ended when all-American offensive guard Sean Farrell fell on a Warner fumble in the end zone and — the ultimate insult — a 91-yard return of a Marino interception by safety Mark Robinson.

"Give Penn State the credit," said Brown. "They outplayed us. They deserved to win. They're a great team. But we're a great team, too."

BLACKLEDGE BESTS MARINO IN BATTLE OF QB'S

By Bob Black

The Pittsburgh Press

He had just finished passing for 262 yards, including two touchdown passes and just one interception in 23 attempts. Yet to Penn State quarterback Todd Blackledge, given the James Coogan Award as the outstanding player in the Pitt-Penn State game, it was not to be construed as a personal victory over the most celebrated quarterback in college football — the Panthers' Danny Marino.

It was merely a 48-14 win over the No. 1-ranked team in the country. The fact that the team happened to be Penn State's biggest rival made it just that much sweeter for the Lions.

A deeply religious player who credits his best performances to "the Lord," Blackledge also proved to be a deeply talented quarterback against Pitt. The 6-foot-3½, 225-pound sophomore from North Canton, Ohio, was every bit the equal of the guy on the other side of the field who has already been named to a number of all-America teams.

"I don't consider this to be an unusual performance for Penn State," Blackledge said of Penn State's most lopsided win over Pitt in 10 years. "People in Pittsburgh see what the Steelers and Pitt have been doing all year and maybe they came to expect the same thing from us.

"But that's not our style. We've been a big-play team when we needed it this season — and I think we proved that today. But in a number of cases we weren't forced to play the kind of game we did today.

"On several of those pass plays we guessed right and they guessed wrong. Sometimes that's the difference between a successful passing game and an unsuccessful one."

In Blackledge's case, it was a matter of guessing right many more times than he guessed wrong.

In the first period, while Pitt was playing a game of pitch and catch that looked as easy as stealing candy from a baby, Penn State unsuccessfully tried its running game, falling behind by 14 points.

But then, looking more innovative than the Ronald Reagan-styled offense people have come to expect from Penn State, Blackledge started doing his thing.

And the more he did it, the better Penn State played, both offensively and defensively.

First it was a 28-yard pass to tight end Mike McCloskey to the Pitt 2, which set up a 2-yard lunge by fullback Mike Meade.

Then it was a 52-yard bomb to wide receiver Kenny Jackson to the Panthers' 8, which Blackledge followed with a quarterback keeper for the tying touchdown.

And from there it just continued to get better for him.

He opened the second half with a 42-yard touchdown pass to Jackson and followed just 2½ minutes later with a 35-yard touchdown pass to the same receiver.

After that it was a 44-yard pass to McCloskey on a drive that ended in a Penn State field goal.

By the fourth period there was no question Blackledge was the man in control. When the Lions needed a first down on a third and long, he would pass for it. When only short yardage was needed, he'd hand off to Curt Warner — whose 104 yards gave him his 11th 100-yard game — Mike Meade or Jon Williams, or he'd get whatever was necessary himself.

"Todd Blackledge has got the makings of a great quarterback," said Penn State coach Joe Paterno. "But then I've said that all year. He's

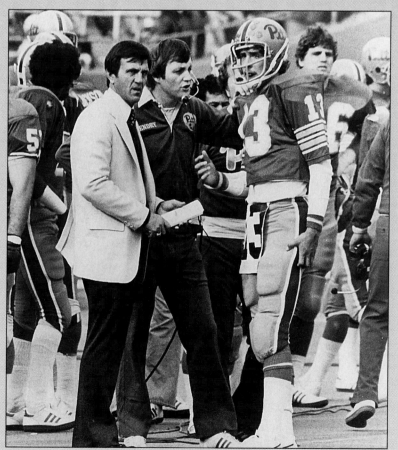

got a great arm and he's a tough kid. He's had a lot of pressure on him this season. But we've played some great defensive teams.

"He also proved to a lot of people how good of a quarterback he was in the Miami game (when he passed for 358 yards, breaking a single-game Penn State passing record). When we weren't able to run on them (Pitt's defense), Todd started hitting the passing game. And that also made our running game work better in the second half."

Blackledge entered the game having passed for 1,295 yards and 10 touchdowns while throwing 13 interceptions. Marino had completed 178 of 294 passes for 2,348 yards and 32 touchdowns, while throwing 17 interceptions.

For one period, Marino made it look easy, quickly riddling Penn State's defense for a pair of touchdown passes. But then Blackledge took over and also made it look easy.

The difference was that when Blackledge got started, Pitt quit, and the result leaves Fiesta Bowl people very happy with a matchup between two 9-2 teams in Penn State and Southern Cal.

Along with the impressive credentials of Warner and Southern Cal's Marcus Allen, they have a quarterback who, in his most important game of the year, outperformed the most impressive college quarterback in the country.

Penn State 26 USC 10

January 1, 1982 | Tempe, Ariz.

Penn State, Warner Run Over Trojans; Allen Held in Check

By Bob Black

The Pittsburgh Press

They had just conquered American's Bowl Team by reducing American's Heisman Trophy winner to mere mortal status. Yet there seemed to be something more important on the minds of the members of perhaps America's most unappreciated college football team.

Easily handling Southern Cal, 26-10, in front of a record Fiesta Bowl crowd of 71,053 rainsoaked fans at Sun Devil Stadium, Penn State held Marcus Allen to just 85 yards on 30 carries.

It was only the second time Allen had been held under 100 yards rushing since taking over as the Trojans' tailback two season's ago. It was also 62 yards below his previous low of the season — 147 yards against Notre Dame.

But as far as Coach Joe Paterno, linebacker Chet Parlavecchio, offensive guard Sean Farrell and a handful of other Nittany Lions were concerned, today's Penn State win over a team with 19 previous bowl victories (more that any other NCAA team) provided a legitimate claim at

Penn State	7	10	9	0 —	26
Southern Cal	7	0	3	0 —	10

being the No. 1 team in the country.

"When you play the kind of schedule we had this season and come out of it as well as we did, then I think you deserve to be considered the best there is," Paterno said. "I felt going into this game that the winner had a legitimate claim at being the best in the country."

Considering that the Lions started with Nebraska, Miami (Fla.), Alabama, Notre Dame, Pitt and finally add Southern Cal to the list of this season's opponents, it might be difficult to question the validity of that statement.

That being the case, the Lions laid unofficial claim to the national title on the strength of the offensive line, which opened holes through which junior tailback Curt Warner rushed for 145 yards and two touch-

Penn State halfback Mike Meade (38) bursts through the middle of the Trojans' line in the second quarter. Meade finished with 60 yards on nine carries.

JOE
PATERNO
ERA

Gregg Garrity (19) leaps into the arms of teammate Mike Meade (38) after catching a touchdown pass in the second quarter.

downs on 26 carries. And a sophomore quarterback, Todd Blackledge, who completed 11 of 14 passes for 175 yards and one touchdown. And a defense, keyed by Parlavecchio and Leo Wisniewski, which held the Trojans to 60 yards rushing, compared to their 299 per game average.

They also did it by taking advantage of five Southern Cal turnovers, which included a pair of fumbles by Allen.

"We were plagued by mistakes all day," said Trojans coach John Robinson. "We didn't run the ball very well. We didn't block very well. And we didn't catch the ball very well, either. I guess we didn't do very many things right.

"But we were beaten by a good football team which played like it wanted to win much more than we did."

That, according to several Penn State players, may have been one of the contributing factors to the Lions' impressive win.

"No way they wanted this football game as much as we did," said Parlavecchio. "Maybe because it wasn't the Rose Bowl, it didn't mean as much to them. I don't know. I do know it meant a lot to us."

That was obvious from the opening series, when the Lions took advantage of USC's first mistake of the game and turned it into a touch-down.

After Allen fumbled a pitch going around his left end, the Lions' Roger Jackson grabbed the loose football at the Trojan 17.

Two plays later, after Blackledge had missed a pass to tight end Vyto Kab in the end zone, Warner went 17 yards off left tackle for the touch-down.

"That came too easy," said Warner. "And, as a result, we really didn't get into the game until that second half. That second half showed how strong this football team can be."

A strong second half became necessary when the Lions failed to take advantage of numerous scoring opportunities in the first half.

The Trojans tied the score in the first quarter when linebacker Chip Banks picked off a Blackledge pass and went 20 yards for the touch-down.

Earlier in the quarter, Lions place-kicker Brian Franco had missed a 36-yard field goal attempt, which he followed with a miss of a 37-yarder in the second quarter.

The Lions grabbed the lead on a 52-yard pass from Blackledge to Gregg Garrity and added three more points when Franco finally hit a field goal — from 21 yards — after Penn State had been stopped at the 9 following a recovery of an Allen fumble by Wisniewski at the Trojans 24.

But, despite owning field advantage for most of the first half, the Lions missed three scoring opportunities during that period — the two missed field goals and their final possession before halftime, when Blackledge failed to plunge in from the 2.

"I was a little concerned," said Blackledge. "We weren't sure what to expect from Southern Cal in the second half. But we didn't panic. We just came out and drove on them to open the second half. That drive was the most important series of the game for us."

The Lions took the ball and drove 80 yards in nine plays — with Blackledge throwing 14 yards to Kab, 15 to Kenny Jackson and seven to Mike McCloskey before Warner carried it in from the 21.

"It was just a quick pitch with the offensive line wiping out the defense," said Warner. "They did a good job of that all day."

But, if Penn State's offense was impressive, its defense was devastating.

"Our defensive scheme wasn't that different than it was in previous games," said Wisniewski, a former high school linebacker and fullback at Fox Chapel, who was named the most valuable defensive player in the game. "We were just more fired up than they were. Physically, we just beat Southern Cal the whole game. That's the only way you can control a team like them."

Though the Trojans added a 37-yard field goal by Steve Jordan, they never really threatened the Lions, who got their final points on a blocked punt by Dave Paffenroth, who knocked it out of the end zone for a safety.

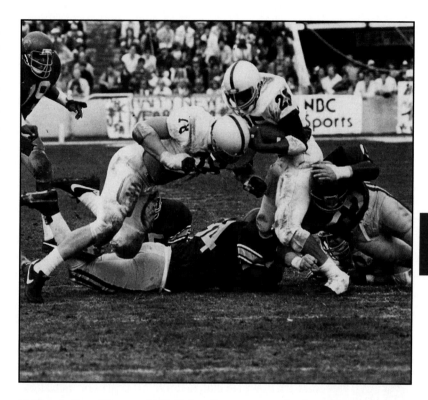

Tailback Curt Warner (25) fights for extra yards during a second-quarter run. Warner ran for 145 yards and scored twice for the Nittany Lions.

"For some reason, we have to keep trying to prove how good a football team we have," said defensive end Rich D'Amico from Central Catholic High School, who finished with nine tackles. "You could tell by their attitude that they really didn't take us that seriously. Any time a team does that, they give us something to prove."

And what they proved was that the Lions may not finish the season ranked No. 1 in the polls, but, of their performance against Southern Cal, there may not have been a team in the country which could have stayed with them today.

JOE PATERNO ERA

127

Penn State 27 Nebraska 24

September 25, 1982 | State College, Pa.

Lions Edge No. 2 Huskers on Dramatic Touchdown Pass

By Dan Donovan

The Pittsburgh Press

Todd Blackledge's last pass was one of his worst, but tight end Kirk Bowman clutched it to his heart one inch above the end zone grass with four seconds left to give Penn State a heart-stopping 27-24 win over No. 2 Nebraska before a record 85,304 fans at Beaver Stadium today.

Quarterback Blackledge put on a spectacular performance, a Heisman Trophy-type performance before a national television audience, driving Penn State 65 yards with 1:18 left in the game.

"Todd's turning into a great leader," Bowman said. "There was a feeling of confidence on the team. We moved 65 yards in 1:18 against a very good team."

Blackledge completed 23 of 39 passes for 295 yards and three touchdowns, tying him for the school record of 15 touchdown passes in a season after only four games.

"This was a good indicator of the character on this football team," Blackledge said. "We rose to the occasion. Defensively, we rose to the

Nebraska	0	7	7	10 —	24
Penn State	7	7	7	6 —	27

occasion to stop their running game. Offensively, we rose to the occasion to establish a running game. This win gives us a lot of confidence for the Alabama game (in two weeks)."

Nebraska appeared to have the game won, driving 80 yards in 13 plays late in the fourth quarter to take a 24-21 lead, Nebraska's first lead of the game.

But a 15-yard personal foul penalty on the ensuing kickoff — an important penalty according to both coaches — gave Blackledge the ball on the 35 and he went to work, calmly leading the Lions up the field, throwing a fourth-and-11 first-down pass to Kenny Jackson and a 15-yard pass to tight end Mike McCloskey — who apparently went out of bounds without landing a foot inbounds — at the Nebraska 2. With

128

JOE
PATERNO
ERA

Nebraska's Kris Van Norman pushes Penn State's Curt Warner (25) out of bounds at the 2-yard line, but Warner scored on a later play.

129

Penn State's Al Harris (88) and Walker Lee Ashley stop Nebraska's Craig Rogers (21).

time ticking away, Blackledge went back and threw to Bowman, a second tight end in short yardage situations.

Bowman, a junior, caught two touchdown passes today — his first two college receptions. Bowman was a defensive end last year, an offensive guard in spring drills and a tight end when the Lions moved Ron Heller to tackle at the start of summer drills. In all, Bowman said, he's played seven positions at Penn State.

"Maybe I've found a home," he said.

Several Cornhuskers disputed the catch, but Bowman said he caught the ball.

"I was concerned the officials weren't going to call it," Bowman said. "I came up with the ball right away and showed it to the official — to show him that I scored."

The ending was probably the most dramatic in Beaver Stadium history and it drove the usually placid fans bananas. After freshman Massimo Manca missed the extra point and the Lions downed the kickoff to end the game, fans flooded the field and the goalpost at the south end — where Bowman scored — was torn down in an instant.

"It was a great football game," Penn State coach Joe Paterno said. "It was a shame that either team had to lose it. There was enough glory in that game for both teams."

Nebraska coach Tom Osborne agreed that "obviously it was a great game for the spectators."

"We played pretty well," Osborne said. "We just couldn't stop their receivers and their quarterback. Their pass protection was good — our coverage wasn't that bad. We had to blitz about 30 percent of the time, more than we like."

The victory was a redemption of sorts for two parts of the Penn State team. The oft-criticized offensive line gave Blackledge scads of time to throw, and the Penn State defense dominated the first half, shutting Nebraska's running game down and forcing quarterback Turner Gill to throw. Gill was up to the challenge, driving the Cornhuskers 80 yards in seven passes at the end of the first half — the only real offense Nebraska generated the first half.

Led by charged up defensive tackle Greg Gattuso, the Lions held Nebraska to 61 yards on the ground in the first half, recovering two of Nebraska's three fumbles.

If Penn State had a fault in the first half, it was not taking a bigger lead than 14-7. Twice in one drive, Blackledge had touchdown passes called back because of a motion penalty and Manca missed field goals of 50,

47 and 34 yards in the first half.

Blackledge's two first-half touchdown drives were vastly different. One went 83 yards in six plays and moved mostly through the air, including a 13-yard pass to Gregg Garrity, a 33-yard bomb to running back Curt Warner and culminated in a 14-yard pass to Bowman. The second traveled 71 yards in six plays and went on the ground, Warner running for 15 yards, breaking a tackle and following a Jon Williams block around end for 31 yards, and scoring his first rushing touchdown of the season from the 2.

Warner gained 78 yards in 13 carries, but missed most of the second half with muscle cramps. Paterno said that Warner, Penn State's Heisman candidate before the season, may have overtrained.

"I think sometimes you can work too hard," Paterno said. "Curt may have worked too hard this summer. I think having a week off (before the Lions play Alabama at Birmingham) should help."

Nebraska played an excellent second half, mixing up the offense and gaining 180 yards rushing and 92 passing.

The teams traded long scoring drives in the third quarter, the Lions moving 83 yards in seven plays, ending in a Blackledge pass right into the gut of wide receiver Jackson. Jackson was surrounded by three defenders and a pass anywhere else might have been intercepted.

But Nebraska, which came into the game aiming for a national championship, outmuscled the Lions for the first time, running mostly behind star center Dave Rimington up the middle, going 80 yards in 15 plays to cut Penn State's lead to 21-14.

Early in the fourth quarter, Lions running back Skeeter Nichols, replacing Warner, fumbled at the Nebraska 44 and Nebraska moved to the 20 before Kevin Seibel kicked a field goal.

Blackledge drove the Lions right back down the field, but was intercepted in the end zone.

Gill masterfully ran the Nebraska offense back up the field, driving it to the touchdown that supposedly would win the game. Except for the spectacular arm of Todd Blackledge.

Penn State quarterback Todd Blackledge (14) completed 23 of 39 passes for 295 yards and 3 touchdowns against Nebraska.

Penn State 19 Pittsburgh 10

November 26, 1982 | State College, Pa.

Lions Weather Pitt, National Title Game vs. Georgia Looms

By Dan Donovan

The Pittsburgh Press

The game, literally, blew in the wind, a wind that Penn State coach and chief amateur meteorologist Joe Paterno made sure his kickers knew well.

Penn State drew a bead on Georgia, the Sugar Bowl and the national championship with a 19-10 win over Pitt that hinged on third-quarter winds that snuffed Pitt's kicking and punting games, but barely affected Penn State's.

Two well-matched and hard-hitting teams battled to a statistical draw — Penn State gained 359 yards, Pitt gained 397 — but Nick Gancitano's four field goals, Ralph Giacommaro's punting and a swirling wind sent Pitt to the Cotton Bowl with a 9-2 record and searching for solace.

Pitt went into the third quarter leading, 7-3, but punter Tony Recchia shanked one 21-yard punt because the wind nearly carried the hike over his head, and punted twice more for 32 and 34 yards.

With the wind in its face, Pitt went into a conservative third-quarter

Pittsburgh	0	7	0	3 —	10
Penn State	3	0	10	6 —	19

offense, throwing only two passes — both dropped — and punting on third down from the end zone. Penn State seized the field position and turned it into 13 points. It was a tribute to the Pitt defense that the Lions didn't score more.

"Pitt let the wind bother it a little more than it should have in the third quarter," Paterno said. "I'm not making a negative comment about them, but we are used to it. We went out Wednesday when it was really windy and cold and we kicked into the wind all day. Then we caught and threw the ball in the wind."

Compared to Wednesday, "today was a pleasure" said Gancitano, a Floridian who kicked field goals of 26, 31, 19 and 29 yards — the last two into the wind and the last in rain, too.

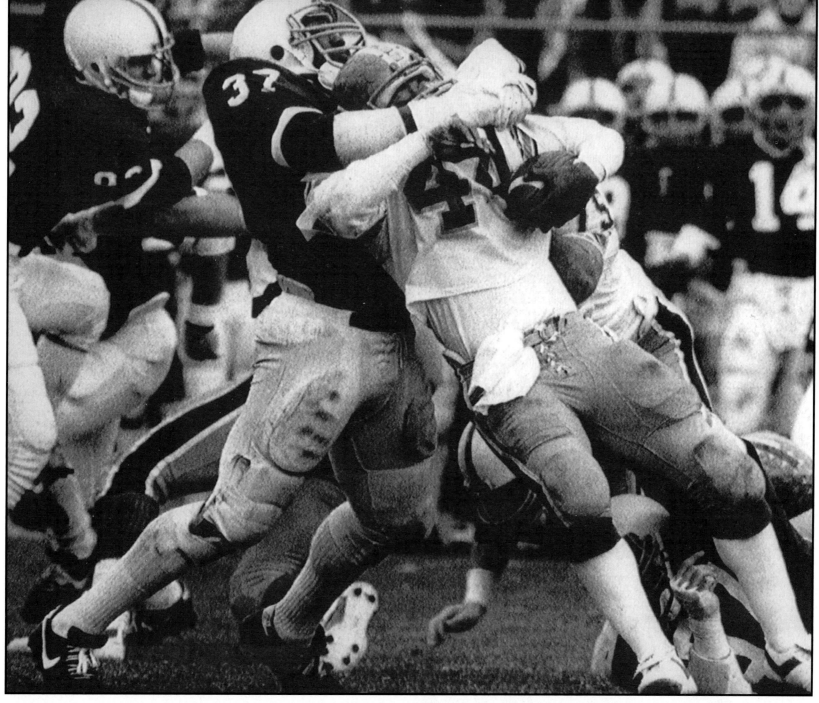

Pitt halfback Bryan Thomas (44) runs into a determined Walker Lee Ashley (37). The Nittany Lions' defense held the Panthers to one touchdown in Penn State's 19-10 victory, which set up a national championship showdown against No. 1 Georgia.

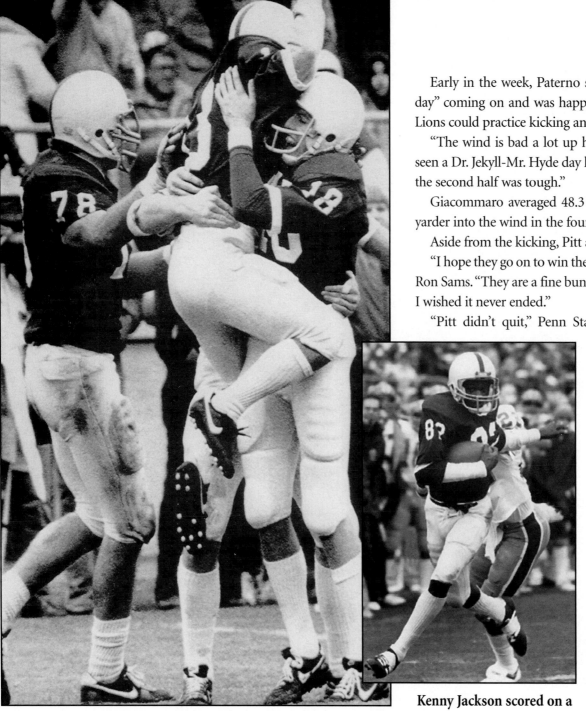

Early in the week, Paterno said he could feel a "typical Penn State day" coming on and was happy that Wednesday was miserable so the Lions could practice kicking and punting into the wind.

"The wind is bad a lot up here," Giacommaro said, "but I've never seen a Dr. Jekyll-Mr. Hyde day like today. It wasn't bad the first half, but the second half was tough."

Giacommaro averaged 48.3 yards on four punts, hitting a low 51-yarder into the wind in the fourth quarter.

Aside from the kicking, Pitt and Penn State were a good match.

"I hope they go on to win the national championship," said Pitt guard Ron Sams. "They are a fine bunch of guys. I enjoyed this game so much, I wished it never ended."

"Pitt didn't quit," Penn State quarterback Todd Blackledge said. "They played hard to the last play. Definitely it was intense, but it wasn't like last year where there was a lot of chit-chat across the line of scrimmage."

Penn State's Curt Warner gained 118 yards on 22 carries, making him the second Penn State runner to gain 1,000 yards two straight years, but was out-gained by Pitt's Bryan Thomas, who gained 143 yards in 31 carries and caught seven passes for 46 yards.

Pitt quarterback Dan Marino completed 18 of 32 passes for 193 yards and one interception, considerably better than Blackledge's 10 of 24 for 149 yards, one touchdown and one interception.

But the No. 2 Lions are 10-1 and will play No. 1 Georgia for the national championship New Year's Day.

Kenny Jackson scored on a 31-yard pass.

Nick Gancitano, center, kicked four field goals against Pitt.

Penn State fans attempted to tear down the goalposts at Beaver Stadium following the game.

"We have one more big one," Blackledge said. "We've had so many big ones, it seems like it never ends, but we've got one more big one left."

Much has been made of Penn State's failure to win a national championship, but Paterno claims the Lions have won three — in 1968, 1969 and 1973, when the Lions went through the regular seasons undefeated and won their bowl games.

"Just because somebody didn't vote you in, doesn't mean you didn't win it," Paterno said. "We blew our shot in 1978 (when the Lions lost to Alabama in the Sugar Bowl), so that makes us 3-1. I hope we don't make it two in a row."

Paterno praised his defense, noting it gave up lots of yardage, but only 10 points.

"They have been maligned, but they have played against some good offensive teams," Paterno said. "We work hard for good field position and try not to give up any easy ones. We have an intelligent defense, and today they played well."

"We always bend, but we never break," said Penn State safety Mark Robinson. "we do that consistently because of the concept of our defense. We play only two down linemen, so we know they'll make a few yards on us. But we try not to let them make any big plays on us."

The Lions gained 210 yards rushing against a Pitt defense that had been ranked third in the nation in rushing defense, giving up only 81.9 yards per game.

"Our offensive line blocked some pretty good defensive linemen," Paterno said. "Nobody else ran that way against Pitt."

Penn State guard Pete Speros said the aggressiveness of the Pitt defensive line, in a way, helped the Lions.

"We would just step into them and let them take us where they wanted to go," Speros said. "That opens big holes."

The Lions used the speed of Warner and Jonathan Williams to run outside, then switched and ran inside the second half.

"In the second half," Warner said, "they were slanting and taking away our outside game, and that opened up the middle. I think they were outside conscious the whole second half."

The Lions threw one interception and fumbled the ball away twice in the first half.

"We were killing ourselves in the first half," Blackledge said. "I knew sooner or later, it would turn around. This team has been through so many tough games, we have a lot of poise and a lot of confidence."

Penn State 27 Georgia 23

January 1, 1983 | New Orleans, La.

Penn State Whips Georgia for First National Championship

By Dan Donovan

The Pittsburgh Press

The Ultimate Contest hasn't happened yet, but this one was pretty darn good, as Penn State survived the well-named tenacious Bulldogs of Georgia, 27-23, before a Sugar Bowl record crowd of 78,124 tonight, to finally reach that Holy Grail, its first undisputed national title.

The Lions led from the moment they took the opening kickoff down the field, and even built up a 20-3 lead, but that didn't tell the story of a bunch of winners, the nation's 1-A team, the Georgia Bulldogs.

The Bulldogs refused to be blown out as a normal team should.

Georgia finally fell to the high-powered, varied Penn State offense and the sure hands of a small, slightly balding walk-on from North Allegheny, wide receiver Gregg Garrity, whose spectacular diving catch on a 47-yard bomb early in the fourth quarter gave the Bulldogs too many points to overcome.

Garrity, streaking down the sideline, made the last game of his college career his best, catching four passes for 116 yards.

Penn State	7	13	0	7 —	27
Georgia	3	7	7	6 —	23

Named the outstanding player of the game was Penn State quarterback Todd Blackledge, who completed 13 of 23 passes for 228 yards, a touchdown, and, most importantly against the leading intercepting team in the nation, no interceptions.

For the second straight year, Penn State running back Curt Warner outgained the Heisman Trophy winner in a bowl game. Despite suffering cramps in his right leg, Warner gained 117 yards on 18 carries for one touchdown.

The gutsiest performance of all may have come from Georgia quarterback John Lastinger, who threw some of the worst passes ever — two were intercepted by Penn State safety Mark Robinson. Yet Lastinger also threw some timely passes, getting the Bulldogs back in the game just as

136

JOE PATERNO ERA

Curt Warner (25) sweeps past Georgia's Terry Hoage on a first-quarter run. Warner finished with 117 yards rushing and two touchdowns.

After coaching three unbeaten teams that did not win national titles, Penn State coach Joe Paterno won the 1982 championship with a once-beaten Nittany Lions team.

it seemed time for them to fold.

Lastinger completed 12 of 27 passes for 166 yards and two touchdowns.

The Lions did not turn over the ball until Kevin Baugh's fumble of a punt in the fourth quarter, a fumble that set up Georgia's last touchdown. The Georgia team lived on turnovers.

Except for the fumble, Baugh had an exceptional night, returning five punts for 106 yards and three kickoffs for 26 yards.

Blackledge calmly, coolly, led the Lions to victory, even though the stunting Georgia defense sacked him five times. The most sacks against the Lions in a game all year had been three.

As the Penn State fans finally got to cheer "We're No. 1" with some conviction, Penn State coach Joe Paterno, long an advocate of a collegiate playoff championship, smiled and said, "I don't think we need a playoff this year — next year we can have a playoff.

"We should be No. 1. With the schedule we played and the people we beat, we should be No. 1. When the No. 1 and No. 2 team play each other, the winner should be No. 1."

Paterno called the Lions his best team ever, his hardest-working team ever, his closest ever. The Lions finished 11-1, losing only to Alabama, 42-21.

"This is the greatest team I've ever played on," Blackledge said. "It has so much character, poise and love for each other. After the loss to Alabama, we just wanted to go out and win every game one at a time. Praise the Lord, it's the greatest season I've ever had."

Although Georgia's secondary "played with a lot of composure," according to Blackledge, he didn't think they "realized how much speed Kenny Jackson and Garrity had."

Fans in the Superdome were treated to a stormy and sensational first half in which the Lions took a 20-10 lead.

Blackledge completed his first five passes, including four for 74 yards as the Lions took the opening kickoff and drove 80 yards for a touchdown.

Blackledge had loads of time to pass, throwing a 33-yarder to tight end Mike McCloskey and a 27-yarder to Garrity. But the touchdown came on a run, as Warner faked into the middle, picked up a block by Joel Coles and went outside to score from two yards out just 2:51 into the game.

Not to be outdone, the Bulldogs drove right down the field, too, though they had to settle for Kevin Butler's 27-yard field goal after a 70-yard, 16-play drive — 40 of those yards gained by Walker.

Aided by four punt returns for 106 yards by Baugh, the Lions kept the offensive pressure on the Bulldogs.

Nick Gancitano kicked a 38-yard field goal set up by a nifty 26-yard run by Warner. Warner beat one man at the line of scrimmage, turned up field and broke another tackle.

Gancitano just missed left on a 47-yard field goal attempt that was set up by Baugh's best punt return of the night, 65 yards through the middle of the field. It wasn't a touchdown only because punter Jim Broadway slowed him down.

Baugh returned the next Georgia punt for 24 yards and Blackledge hit Garrity going down the sideline with a 36-yard pass. Four plays later, on third and a half-yard at the 9, Warner stepped into the middle of the Georgia line, stopped, changed directions and scored to give the Lions a 17-3 lead.

JOE PATERNO ERA

The fired-up Lions bottled up the Bulldogs at the 8 on the kickoff and quickly forced another punt, setting up a 45-yard Gancitano field goal with only 44 seconds left in the half.

But Georgia wasn't about to give up. Herschel Walker ran the kickoff back 23 yards and Lastinger threw five straight passes, completing four, the first time he passed successfully in the first half.

At the 36, Lastinger passed to wide receiver Kevin Harris who, as he was tackled by Lions cornerback Dan Biondi, lateraled to Walker, who gained 10 more yards to the 10.

On the next play, Lastinger threw high in the end zone to Herman Archie, who had dropped several passes early in the game.

The 6-foot-5 Archie outjumped 5-9 Biondi for the ball and the touchdown with five seconds left in the half to make it 20-10.

The Bulldogs marched down 69 yards in 11 plays on the opening drive of the second half to cut the Penn State lead to 20-17.

Early in the fourth quarter, the bomb to Garrity gave the Lions their 27-17 lead.

"That was a big factor in our regaining our momentum," Paterno said. "It was a typical Blackledge performance. He is poised, confident and can come back from adversity."

Later, Baugh, who should have played it safe and called a fair catch while fielding a punt on his own 43, fumbled the ball and Georgia recovered. Lastinger then drove the Bulldogs 43 yards in six plays, passing to tight end Clarence Kay for a touchdown. The Lions stopped Walker's attempted sweep for the two-point conversion.

With 3:53 left, the Lions took the kickoff and sat on the ball, slowly moving up the field until time ran out as a Ralph Giacomarro punt bounced into the end zone.

"Penn State played like champions," said Walker, who was held to 22 yards in the second half. "They took advantage of their opportunities and we didn't take advantage of ours."

National Title Sounds Sweet to Penn State

By Pat Livingston

The Pittsburgh Press

That elusive national championship, a thorn in Coach Joe Paterno's side for the last 15 years, may finally be headed to State College this week, the result of Penn State's 27-23 victory over No. 1-ranked Georgia before a record Sugar Bowl crowd of 78,124 in the Louisiana Superdome last night.

Only a decision by a panel of football coaches and another by a group sportswriters stand in the way of a declaration that Penn State, on its fourth try, is indeed the national champion. That decision should be forthcoming this week.

The alternative is unbeaten Southern Methodist, the only unbeaten major college team in the country, whose 11-0-1 record includes an unimpressive 7-3 victory over Pitt, the Lions' arch-rivals, in the Cotton Bowl six hours earlier.

For a time tonight, it appeared Paterno would have little trouble in capturing the title which had eluded him for so long as Penn State, powered by the passing of quarterback Todd Blackledge, piled up an easy 20-3 lead in the second period.

But a sudden rally by Georgia, which netted the loser two touchdowns in a five-minute stretch spanning the second and third periods, put the Bulldogs back in the game, 20-17.

And with the ever-dangerous Herschel Walker, a game-breaker if ever there was one, in the Georgia backfield, that was a perilous position for Paterno, indeed.

However, just as it appeared that the momentum, which had swung away with Georgia's rally 20 minutes earlier, was about to desert Penn State, Blackledge came up with the game's key play.

It was a 48-yard pass to his wide receiver, Gregg Garrity, who had a step on Georgia cornerback Tony Flack as he crossed the goal line. Garrity made a diving catch for a touchdown, putting Penn State in front 27-17.

There were four minutes left in the game when Georgia challenged again, getting down to the Penn State 10-yard line, largely on the passing of underrated John Lastinger, the Bulldogs' quarterback. One of Lastinger's wobbly passes, on third down, found its way into the arms of Clarence Kay, narrowing the count with 3:54 left.

Penn State stopped a two-point conversion attempt. Georgia, instead of needing a field goal to win as it would have had the conversion been successful, now needed a touchdown. Georgia trailed by four, 27-23.

The Lions were to control the ball, not giving it up until they punted into the end zone on the last play of the game.

Of course, championships have never been a thing with Paterno. Although Penn State did not win a national championship in his first 16 years as coach, he never allowed such a failing to develop into paranoia.

Throughout his coaching career, his teams set their own standards. How they fared, not how many titles they won, was the big thing with Paterno.

"I never cared much about championships," said Paterno, "except as they affected the young men who played on those teams. I was always satisfied when we won football games, which was our purpose in the sport.

"It never bothers me that people still think we didn't win any championships. I coached three undefeated, untied teams — and one of them won 22 games in a row. There were champions as far as I was concerned. I didn't care what the rest of the country thought."

The teams Paterno referred to were the Penn State team of 1968, which won 11 straight games, the only team to do that in the country, and then whipped Kansas, the Big Eight champion, 15-14, in the Orange Bowl.

The best Paterno's team could get that year was a second-place rating by United Press International, and a third-place finish by The Associated Press.

The following year, Penn State again went 12-0-0, extending what was to become a 31-game unbeaten streak, but again the Lions were ignored in the ratings.

Paterno's third perfect season came in 1973, a year when there were seven unbeaten teams in the country at the end of the regular season. Despite the past slights, however, nobody yet was taking Penn State seriously.

Penn State's Mike McCloskey leaps over Georgia's Tony Flack (8) for a reception.

Penn State 34 Alabama 28

Lions Upset No. 3 Alabama, Husker Controversy Recalled

JOE
PATERNO
ERA

By Mike DeCourcy

The Pittsburgh Press

Many football fans, particularly those not swearing allegiance to anyone calling himself a "Cornhusker," said the 1982 Penn State-Nebraska game would never be equaled for excitement in college football. They were wrong.

Not only was it equaled today, it was practically repeated.

There were only a few differences. It was Alabama playing Penn State, the disputed pass reception took a different form and the game left 4-1 Alabama in position to make a comeback run at the national championship.

But it was at Beaver Stadium, there was a beyond-capacity crowd, CBS had it on television and the game began at 3:45 under temporary lights. The most important thing that didn't change was the winning team. That was Penn State, 34-28.

Penn State (3-3) used Doug Strang's 241 passing yards and D.J. Dozier's 165 yards rushing to open a 34-7 lead after three periods, but

Alabama	7	0	0	21	— 28
Penn State	14	3	17	0	— 34

No. 3 Alabama constructed a magnificent rally behind quarterback Walter Lewis, who led the Crimson Tide to three fourth-quarter touchdowns and passed for 336 yards.

Alabama compiled 598 total yards but could not make it 600 on the final play of the game. Penn State tackle Greg Gattuso stopped freshman tailback Kerry Goode from the State 2 as time ran out.

"You think of ways to get back in it. You ask yourself, 'Are you going to give up or fight to win?'" said Lewis. "We put ourselves into the situation. We had to go bail ourselves out."

Lewis, the guy with the biggest bucket, helped Alabama cut the Penn State advantage to six points with 5:36 remaining when he hit flanker Jesse Bendross with an 8-yard TD pass. Alabama got the ball back with

Penn State defenders Brad Harris (34) and Harry Hamilton (17) apply pressure to Alabama quarterback Walter Lewis. The Crimson Tide suffered three fumbles and three interceptions.

JOE
PATERNO
ERA

143

DID HE OR DIDN'T HE? Alabama tight end Preston Gothard latches on to the ball and falls out of the end zone late in the fourth quarter. Officials ruled Gothard did not have possession of the ball when he went out of bounds, preserving the Lions' lead.

nearly three minutes left when Stan Gay blocked Nick Gancitano's 43-yard field goal attempt and recovered it at the Alabama 49.

The situation looked familiar. Penn State had spoiled Nebraska's day by coming from behind for a 27-24 victory last fall. Alabama was set to do the same to the Nittany Lions.

"Yeah, it's funny how I was thinking this time last year that we won it in the last two seconds," said Paterno. "Were they going to do it this year with that great comeback they had?"

"Everyone was real confident in the huddle," said Crimson Tide receiver Joey Jones. "I knew we were going to score."

Alabama moved straight toward the goal line, Lewis completing four passes for 30 yards to move the Tide to the Penn State 12. On third down, freshman Kerry Goode carried for six yards and a first down.

Alabama had four plays from the six and enough time — 28 seconds — to get them all off.

First down was an incomplete pass. So was second down. Lewis scrambled for two yards on third down. Fourth down was an incomplete pass.

But not an ordinary incomplete pass. Penn State was offside on the play, which gave Alabama one more shot. Alabama's players figured they didn't need it.

Preston Gothard apparently caught Lewis' four-yard pass for the winning TD, but he juggled the ball at the top of his jump and back judge Walter Lucas ruled that Gothard didn't have possession when his body hit the end line.

"I thought I had it. The referee said I didn't have it. His judgment is what counts," Gothard said.

Gattuso's big play followed, when Alabama elected to run a "Toss-28" to Goode instead of passing, Gattuso shot the gap off right tackle and nailed Goode for no gain.

"We had not gained less than seven yards on that play all day in the same situation, against the same defense," Alabama coach Ray Perkins said. "(Their defense was) lined up like you'd like 'em to line up. We just didn't execute."

That was Alabama's problem all day.

The Crimson Tide lost three fumbles and three interceptions, all at the wrong time, as Penn State finally got a taste of good fortune.

In the first period, Penn State scored on an 80-yard TD pass from Doug Strang to tight end Dean DiMidio when two Alabama defenders — Freddie Robinson and David Valletto — allowed DiMidio to get behind them and misplayed Strang's floating pass.

That tied the game at 7-7, Alabama having opened the scoring with an 88-yard drive, capped by Lewis' eight-yard pass to Jones, that showed the Tide could dominate Penn State with its ground game.

They just couldn't hang onto the ball.

Penn State took Linnie Patrick's fumble and turned it into a 38-yard scoring pass from Strang to Kenny Jackson with his 27-yard run. Dozier went over the 100-yard mark for the fourth straight game with a 64-yarder that set up his own one-yard score.

A Gancintano 39-yard field goal with 6:31 left in the third quarter gave Penn State a 27-point lead and had the record crowd of 85,614 screaming.

"I thought we had it wrapped up," Paterno said. "I guess we played it too conservatively."

Alabama came back quickly and ferociously. Lewis led touchdown drives of 87, 69 and 78 yards, handed to Goode for one TD and completed two scoring passes to Bendross to get the Tide back into the game.

The comeback turned a rout into a classic.

"One of the best games I've ever been associated with?" said Perkins, tersely repeating a question. "Hell no. We lost the game."

Penn State running back D.J. Dozier rushed for 165 yards against the Crimson Tide defense.

JOE PATERNO ERA

Penn State 23 Alabama 3

Lions Rip No. 2 Alabama, Tide Musters Only One FG

By Mike DeCourcy

The Pittsburgh Press

When the Penn State Nittany Lions beat Alabama a year ago, they couldn't escape the inevitable questions about Miami. It was a lot like that today, but this time everyone was talking about the university, not the city.

Will No. 6 Penn State get an opportunity to play No. 1 Miami in some sort of national championship bowl game, as it did Oklahoma in the Orange Bowl last season? Tough question. Do they deserve the chance? Got anyone better for the Hurricanes to play?

Penn State (7-0) proved beyond a reasonable doubt there are few better teams in college football, sticking a 23-3 defeat into the craws of No. 2 Alabama and the silent majority of the 60,210 fans in Bryant-Denny Stadium. With No. 4 Nebraska also losing, Penn State figures to move up at least two, and possibly three spots in The Scripps-Howard poll.

"Someone has to play awfully well to beat us the way we're playing,"

Penn State	0	14	3	6 —	23
Alabama	3	0	0	0 —	3

Coach Joe Paterno said, adding later, "I knew we were ready. I think we were a little stronger today. It was two good teams; we just played a little better.

Penn State played about as perfectly as possible. The offensive linemen protected quarterback John Shaffer as if he were holding their lunch money, permitting the Crimson Tide one sack, on a meaningless fourth-quarter play. All-American linebacker Cornelius Bennett made 13 tackles but never came close enough to Shaffer to read his number.

The Penn State defensive front, linebackers included, hounded Tide quarterback Mike Shula into one of his worst days, a 14-for-30, 172-yard disaster. Shula was sacked five times, twice each by Tim Johnson and Brentwood's Don Graham, and once by Freeport's Bob White.

Kicker Massimo Manca, center, celebrates his fourth-quarter field goal that put the Nittany Lions in front, 20-3.

Tim Johnson (55) lost his helmet after sacking Alabama quarterback Mike Shula.

The powerful Alabama running game was good for just 87 yards, the tailback tandem of Bobby Humphrey (27 yards) and Gene Jelks (15) rendered ineffective. Penn State linebacker Trey Bauer had an outstanding day, making nine tackles, causing a fumble and recovering another.

The Tide lost three fumbles, Penn State one.

The Lions secondary held speedy Al Bell to one catch for 4 yards. The speedier Greg Richardson got loose for four catches and 60 yards, but nothing longer than 22. Cornerback Eddie Johnson and safety Ray Isom each intercepted a pass.

There's more.

Kicker Massimo Manca, who was hitting .333 in 1986 (3-for-9), converted field goals of 37, 29 and 42 yards, the only points of the second half. He's up to .500.

Shaffer, a 40-percent passer in road games, completed 13 of 17 attempts (77 percent) for 168 yards and was not intercepted. He completed seven of eight attempts in the second half.

"We didn't get good pressure on their quarterback. If the quarterback has time to throw, I'm not surprised if he completes passes," Alabama coach Ray Perkins said. "But Shaffer's not the guy who makes their offense go. It's those backs, those Doziers and Smiths and Manoas and Clarks."

With Alabama a 6-point favorite, the game was supposed to go one way, but quickly went the other. As did Penn State's most effective offensive plays.

"We wanted to run a lot of counter plays to keep them off balance," Lions center Keith Radecic said. "They're great players, but because they're so quick, they overrun a lot of plays."

For the same reason, Penn State's running backs, including D.J. Dozier (63 yards rushing) and reserve Blair Thomas (57), were encouraged by their coaches to cut back against the flow when the opportunity seemed ripe. They compiled 210 rushing yards against an Alabama defense that previously allowed an average of 97.9.

"Anybody we play, that's what we think: We'll run right at them, until they stop us," said Fran Ganter, Penn State's offensive coordinator. "We're a power football team, and we have to make our kids believe in that."

JOE PATERNO ERA

Alabama played that role in the first quarter, using three running plays to reach the Penn State 49 on the opening series. One the fourth, however, fullback Bo Wright was hit by White and fumbled, and Duffy Cobbs recovered for Penn State.

Alabama got it back and mixed the same strategy with a 31-yard pass from Shula to Humphrey. That set up Van Tiffin's 41-yard field goal, the Tide's only score, to make it 3-0.

Penn State was stopped on its first two series, but the third time was a harm to the Alabama defense. Dozier gained 24 yards on a screen pass, rushed for gains of 3 and 7 yards, then broke for a 19-yard touchdown run five seconds into the second quarter.

"I was a little nervous when they stuffed us twice at the beginning," Shaffer said. "It was just a matter of keeping our composure."

Thomas, in to give Dozier a breather, did similar damage to Alabama two series later, gaining 16 and 29 yards on draw plays and then scoring on a 3-yard reverse.

Penn State led at halftime, 14-3.

"They got after us. They were the better team today," Alabama center Wes Neighbors said. "There was no doubt from the third quarter on who was going to win the game."

Penn State 14 Miami 10

January 2, 1987 | Tempe, Ariz.

Lions Pound Miami in Fiesta, Claim 2nd National Title

JOE PATERNO ERA

By Mike DeCourcy

The Pittsburgh Press

Penn State	0	7	0	7 —	14
Miami	0	7	0	3 —	10

Most of the emotion was spent on the moment, in the 90 seconds or so it took to clear the fanatics from the field at Sun Devil Stadium. Had to get those last nine seconds in. Had to be official.

So John Shaffer knelt down, cradling the football, and it was done. Penn State 14, Miami 10. The Nittany Lions had No. 1 all to themselves. It was numbing, frankly.

How does one deal with perfection? And that is what this was. Not just 12-0 and Penn State's second national championship, but the fulfillment of every goal the Lions had established for both tonight's game and the entire season.

Tailback D.J. Dozier and linebacker Shane Conlan sat calmly near the rear entrance of the press tent afterward, awaiting their awards as offensive and defensive MVP's, smiling that unique smile of disbelief. They talked some about what it felt like to win what was billed as the greatest game ever played in college football and ended up, in retrospect, under-

played. The consensus: They'd have to check the films.

"We were just sitting there talking like, 'Yeah, we won.' It hasn't hit me," Conlan said. "Maybe tomorrow." Dozier's expression was blank.

Fine. The talk of this Fiesta Bowl, the most super bowl ever consummated in college football, will subside in no great hurry.

This became the Lions' second national title in five years, the first coming in 1982, and the fourth time in Coach Joe Paterno's 21 seasons they finished the season unbeaten.

A record crowd of 73,098 in the stadium and a large NBC television audience watched. The network helped move the game to prime time to showcase the showdown between No. 1 and No. 2, between Heisman Trophy winner Vinny Testaverde and his latest victims.

JOE PATERNO ERA

Lions halfback Blair Thomas (32) is corralled by Miami's Freddy Highsmith.

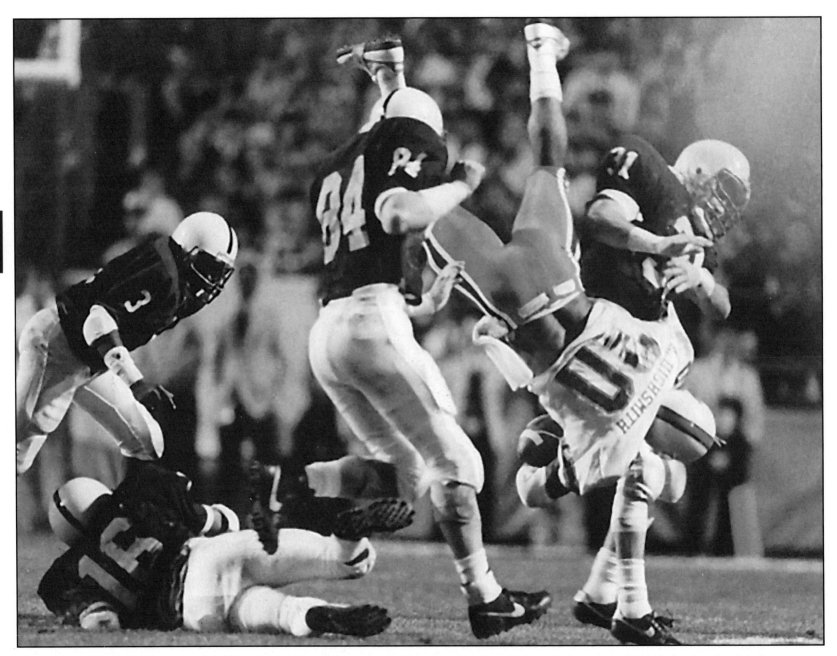

152 Miami tailback Alonzo Highsmith is sent airborne by Penn State's Shane Conlan (31) and Keith Karpinski (84) during the third quarter.

Testaverde fulfilled most of the requirements for victory, leading his team to 445 yards and 22 first downs and completing 26 of 50 for 285 yards. Not much in the way of points, though, and there were those interceptions. All five of them.

Particularly the last.

"There was just no way we could lose this game," senior linebacker Trey Bauer said. "The whole season, the way we've been getting out of situations ... everybody just sucked it up. We couldn't lose."

The end couldn't have been more fitting for Penn State, nor caused more fits for Miami. It came down to the penultimate play, fourth-and-goal from the Penn State 13 with 18 seconds left, and Miami's only hope for victory was to cross the goal line. Falling short of a touchdown meant falling short.

Penn State had permitted the Hurricanes, trailing by four, to drive 71 yards in the final three minutes, from their 23 to within 6 yards of the winning points. And then, as had happened to Notre Dame before them, the Hurricanes backward march began.

An incomplete pass first, and then Tim Johnson nearly tore off Testaverde's head with a 7-yard sack. Testaverde underthrew on third down, missing Warren Williams at the 2. On fourth down, Testaverde found Pete Giftopoulos near the goal line for the second time.

Giftopoulos plays linebacker for Penn State. His second interception clinched the victory, and the players and fans celebrated wildly on the field. When it was cleared up, the matter of the final seconds was too.

"We spent an awful lot of the football game playing pass defense inside the 30," Paterno said. "We have been awfully tough down inside the 20-yard line. And we play with confidence down there."

It was the ultimate challenge for the Penn State defense, a unit that had conquered everything but. They gave a magnificent performance under dire, but familiar circumstances. The offense was, if not dead, then sleeping soundly. It produced just eight first downs and 162 yards and ran only 59 plays to Miami's 93.

Under normal circumstances, NBC would have presented to the

JOE PATERNO ERA

Coach Joe Paterno gives some last-minute instructions to his defense from the sidelines.

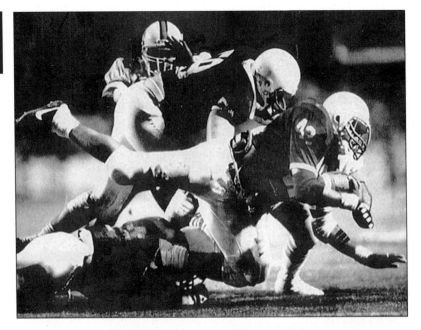

The Nittany Lions' D.J. Dozier worked hard for his 99 yards and one touchdown. Dozier also had two receptions in Penn State's Fiesta Bowl victory over Miami.

Penn State linebacker Don Graham (53) celebrates sacking Miami quarterback Vinny Testaverde.

nation the throbbing rock beat of a "Miami Vice" rerun in this time slot. What the Fiesta Bowl almost provided was the throbbing headache of a Penn State rerun from the 1986 Orange Bowl, when the Lions lost last season's national championship to Oklahoma because the offense could not complement a superb defensive effort.

"Their rush was so good, we never had any time to get into what we wanted to do. We just couldn't double everybody up," Paterno said.

With Miami blitzing often and four times sacking Shaffer, he had time on only 5 of 16 attempts, the completions covering 53 yards. D.J. Dozier gained 99 yards on 20 carries, but the rest of the Penn State running game was largely ineffective, producing 109 yards.

It did produce one solid drive, however, 74 yards in 10 plays toward a 4-yard touchdown run by Shaffer to tie the game at 7-7 with 1:49 left in the first half. Shaffer hit Eric Hamilton with a 23-yard pass over the middle on third-and-12, and Tim Manoa's 20-yard run put Shaffer in position for the touchdown.

Miami had earlier gone ahead on 1-yard run by halfback Melvin Bratton, set up by an odd fumble/interception by Shaffer plucked out of the air by defensive end Bill Hawkins.

Miami's offense never drove for a touchdown. It moved the ball, but on Penn State's terms. All-American wideout Michael Irvin and Brian Blades were near silent before Miami's final drive, and Brett Perriman never became a factor. Miami receivers dropped at least a half-dozen passes.

Testaverde said it might have been the change in weather or atmosphere, but finally declared, "There was no reason for it."

Really, there was. Penn State cornerbacks Duffy Cobbs and Eddie Johnson played so far off the receivers they could barely read Miami's jersey numbers, but that kept the Hurricanes from breaking big plays, and it gave the Lions running starts for some nasty, vicious hits.

"A couple of hits like that," Bauer said, "and their receivers' arms seemed to get about 8 inches shorter."

Penn State and Miami were still early in the final quarter, as both Mark Seelig of the Hurricanes (28 yards) and Massimo Manca of Penn State (49) missed field goals. Seelig connected on a 38-yarder with 11:49 remaining and gave Miami a 10-7 lead.

Penn State took the kickoff, sputtered, and gave the ball back to Miami. "I told the defense, 'Just one more time, and the offense will get you out of it,'" Paterno said. "They were tired of waiting."

On second-and-10 from his 34, Testaverde dropped back and looked toward tight end Alfredo Roberts. He passed, but toward Conlan, who made his second interception and returned it to the 5. One play later, Dozier had a touchdown run and Penn State had all the points it needed.

Call It Unanimous: Penn State Voted No. 1

There are no doubts that Penn State, which finished its season with a 12-0 record by defeating Miami, 14-10, in the Fiesta Bowl Friday night, is the nation's No. 1 college team.

In four polls announced yesterday, Penn State was named No. 1. Only in one of the polls were the Nittany Lions not a unanimous choice.

Penn State received all 31 first- place votes and 620 points in the final Scripps Howard poll, selected by sportswriters. Miami, which led virtually all year, finished second in the poll with 582 points. Orange Bowl winner Oklahoma, a loser to Miami in September, was third (564).

In the United Press International poll, Penn State swept all 49 ballots cast by the UPI Board of Coaches, receiving 735 points. Miami finished second with 673 points and third place Oklahoma got 660.

Only The Associated Press poll, selected by sportswriters, was not unanimous. Penn State was voted No. 1 with 1,137 points — three shy of unanimous — to 1,064 for Miami. Oklahoma which received the other three first-place votes, was third with 1,045.

The Football Writers Association of America awarded Penn State the Grantland Rice Trophy, symbolic of its No. 1 designation.

Penn State 24 Notre Dame 21

November 17, 1990 | Notre Dame, Ind.

Sacca Passes Nittany Lions Past No. 1 Notre Dame

By Mike DeCourcy

The Pittsburgh Press

College football's national championship race was thrown into disarray with Penn State's 24-21 victory against top-ranked Notre Dame today.

For a change "thrown" is not an inappropriate verb to use in connection with a Penn State victory.

Quarterback Tony Sacca completed 20 of 34 pass attempts for three touchdowns and a career-best 277 yards as the Lions shocked a crowd of 59,075 at Notre Dame Stadium.

"Tony grew up today," Coach Joe Paterno said.

Sacca's 14-yard touchdown pass to tight end Al Golden tied the score with 7:15 remaining, and freshman Craig Fayak of Belle Vernon then won the game with a 34-yard field goal with four seconds left.

The victory was the eighth in a row for No. 18 Penn State (8-2), which could reach the Top 10 off this upset. Notre Dame (8-2) is likely to fall from it precarious perch atop the polls, with Colorado, Miami, BYU and Georgia Tech eager to replace it. A change at the No. 1 spot would be the

Penn State	7	0	7	10	— 24
Notre Dame	14	7	0	0	— 21

sixth this season.

"It's hard to describe the feeling," said tailback Leroy Thompson, who ran for 56 yards and caught seven passes for another 83. "Everybody was hugging each other, and there were guys crying … I was crying."

Penn State had wanted to wait until after this game before making a decision on a bowl, but the rush by bowls and schools to wrap up deals last weekend left the Nittany Lions out of the New Year's Day spotlight and with a Dec. 28 game against Florida State in the Blockbuster Bowl.

Even with the Sugar Bowl possibly dumping Virginia, Athletic Director Jim Tarman said the Lions would not renege on their commitment to the Blockbuster.

"We've still got a big game against Pitt, and that's all I want to think

Penn State kicker Craig Fayak boots the winning kick against the Fighting Irish.

JOE
PATERNO
ERA

about," Paterno said. "We've got a good matchup, one of the better matchups."

Penn State had to rally from deficits of 14-0 and 21-7, but its defense held the Irish scoreless and permitted only 76 yards in the second half. Paterno said his secondary was giving too much room to the Notre Dame receivers in the first half and playing more aggressively was the key to turning around the game.

All-America receiver Raghib Ismail did not play for Notre Dame in the second half because of a thigh injury, after gaining 109 yards in the first 30 minutes.

"No doubt we have built our offense around him," Couch Lou Holtz said, "But you have to rise to the occasion."

After Notre Dame built its lead in the first quarter on a 22-yard touchdown run by Ricky Watters

Tony Sacca completed 20 of 34 pass attempts for three TD's and 277 yards.

Joe Paterno celebrates the win over the Irish with Lions fans..

Notre Dame receiver Raghib Ismail (25) did not play in second half against the Lions due to an injury.

and a 12-yard run by Tony Brooks, Sacca threw a 32-yard score to Terry Smith on a fake reverse play to make it 14-7.

Notre Dame took a 21-7 lead into halftime after an overpowering 92-yard drive capped by quarterback Rick Mirer's 1-yard drive.

Mirer, who finished 8 of 21 for 161 yards, threw two second-half interceptions that set up Penn State scores.

The first was picked off by Mark D'Onofrio in the third quarter and returned 38 yards. Sacca followed with his 11-yard touchdown toss to tight end Rick Sayles.

Penn State drove toward a tie with two big passes, and then Sacca threw his touchdown to Golden.

With the score, 21-21, and Penn State facing fourth-and-2 at the ND 37, Paterno elected to punt with 2:35 remaining. Doug Helkowski's kick pinned the Irish at their 7.

They got one first down, but on a third-down play, Mirer overthrew split end Tony Smith and found Lions strong safety Darren Perry. Perry intercepted at the 39 and returned it to the Irish 19 to set up Fayak's kick.

JOE PATERNO ERA

159

Penn State 31 Michigan 24

October 15, 1994 | Ann Arbor, Mich.

Collins Passes Lions to Victory on Road to Rose Bowl

By Marino Parascenzo

Pittsburgh Post-Gazette

Penn Sate's unbeaten Nittany Lions blew a 16-0 lead but came up smelling like roses — possible the Rose Bowl variety — with a gripping 31-24 victory over the Michigan Wolverines.

The Lions broke from a 24-24 tie with a lightning touchdown — quarterback Kerry Collins' 16-yard strike to receiver Bobby Engram with just under three minutes to play.

It was Penn State's biggest win in two years in the Big Ten, and came before 106,832, the third-largest crowd ever in Michigan Stadium and the third-largest in NCAA history.

The two had opened like a pair of old Southwest Conference gunslinger teams, then settled down into a Big Ten power bash that wasn't resolved until Lions linebacker Willie Smith set the stage for the winning drive, blitzing like a demon from the right side to nail Michigan quarterback Todd Collins on a third-and-3 at the Michigan 28.

Michigan had to punt.

Penn State	10	6	8	7 —	31
Michigan	0	3	14	7 —	24

And that was followed immediately by a fierce and winning Penn State drive that found the right cracks in the Michigan defense.

The drive went 55 yards in five plays, beginning with Collins hitting receiver Engram for 14 yards, and ending with Engram running that devilish slant pattern from the right, coasting into wide-open country between two distant defenders, and taking Collins' 16-yard strike for the winning touchdown at 2:53.

The road to the Rose Bowl is still under construction but it looks a bit more open now.

It's heresy in the Big Ten to talk about the national championship. All eyes remain fixed on the Rose Bowl.

"But we want to go to Pasadena and win the national championship,"

Carter said, "And we think we can do both."

The victory keeps third-ranked Penn State unbeaten at 6-0 and drops No. 5 Michigan to 4-2. But the Big Ten records are more to the point at the moment, and Penn State is alone atop the conference with a 3-0 record. Michigan is 2-1, and Purdue, after tying Wisconsin, is 2-0-1.

"We beat a great team," Penn State coach Joe Paterno said. "They put a lot of pressure on us. I was extremely concerned about our missed chances. I knew Michigan wasn't bad, and that they'd come out hard. I was very concerned at the half."

Penn State rushed for 213 yards — 165 by tailback Ki-Jana Carter, splinted right thumb and all — and Kerry Collins passed for 231 yards, piling up a 444 total against Michigan's 437.

The Lions opened not with the

Joe Paterno consoles Michigan coach Gary Moeller after the Lions' 31-24 victory in Ann Arbor.

same numbers but with the equivalent authority of those five blowout games against lesser opponents. That is, they scored the first three times they had the ball.

The first was a 24-yard field goal by Brett Conway on the opening possession for a 3-0 lead. Then Collins hitting tight end Keith Olsommer on a three-yard pass for a 10-0 lead at the end of the first quarter. Then two more field goals by Conway, a 28-yarder early in the

second period — set up by linebacker Jason Collins stripping the ball from tailback Tim Biakabutuka — and a 29-yarder with 5:52 left in the half.

Though considerably muted — those were not all TD's — it looked like business as usual for the club that had been outscoring opponents by a cumulative 89-12 in the first period and 87-30 in the second.

Michigan managed a field goal on the final play of the first half, Remy

Hamilton's 33-yarder set up by Penn State punter Joe Jurevicius' weak 28-yard punt, and linebacker Brian Gelzheiser spearing a fallen Todd Collins, the 15-yard penalty which give Michigan a first down and new life.

The Lions were looking good, though, with a 16-3 lead at the half.

But you can keep lightning in the bottle for only so long, and that was the case with Michigan tailback Tyrone Wheatley.

The Lions had pretty well shut him down. He got zero yards on his first two carries in the first period, and by halftime he had accumulated the dizzying total of 11 yards on nine carries, an average of 1.2.

Then it was his turn to do the dizzying. He got one yard with the first carry, opening the third quarter, then boom.

On second down, he whipped around right end, beat Gelzheiser wide, and raced untouched 67 yards for the touchdown, cutting Michigan's deficit to 16-10.

Then Jurevisius shanked a 16-yarder on Penn State's next possession, and Michigan was in sweet position, at their own 49.

Then boom-boom-boom.

Todd Collins hit split end Amani Toomer for 30 yards, to the Lions 21, and after an incomplete pass, Wheatley took a pitchout and swept wide the rest of the way to the TD and Michigan's only lead of the game, 17-16.

The Lions retook the lead on the next possession, going 80 yards in 10 plays, with Kerry Collins throwing his third TD pass, an 8-yarder to fullback Jon Witman. Then Collins hit receiver Freddie Scott for a two-point conversion and a 24-17 lead.

The two-pointer came in handy when Michigan scored on Biakabutuka's 2-yard smash on fourth down with 11:37 left in the game. Moeller opted for the comfort of a tying extra point, and Hamilton kicked it for the 24-24 deadlock. Both teams were playing for time now.

Michigan still had some life, and nearly three minutes to enjoy it.

But they weren't done making mistakes yet. Hamilton missed a chip-shot field goal in the first quarter; Toomer dropped an easy pass back in the second quarter to be followed by Kraig Baker's feeble 23-yard punt, setting up a Lions field goal, and so forth.

This time, with 2:16 left, Toomer had beaten the defenders and was under full speed at about the Lions 3, and Todd Collins fired from the 50. But Toomer stayed to the left, and the ball was about two yards to his right.

He had made seven catches for 157 yards, but he missed the biggest catch of the day.

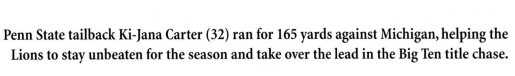

Penn State tailback Ki-Jana Carter (32) ran for 165 yards against Michigan, helping the Lions to stay unbeaten for the season and take over the lead in the Big Ten title chase.

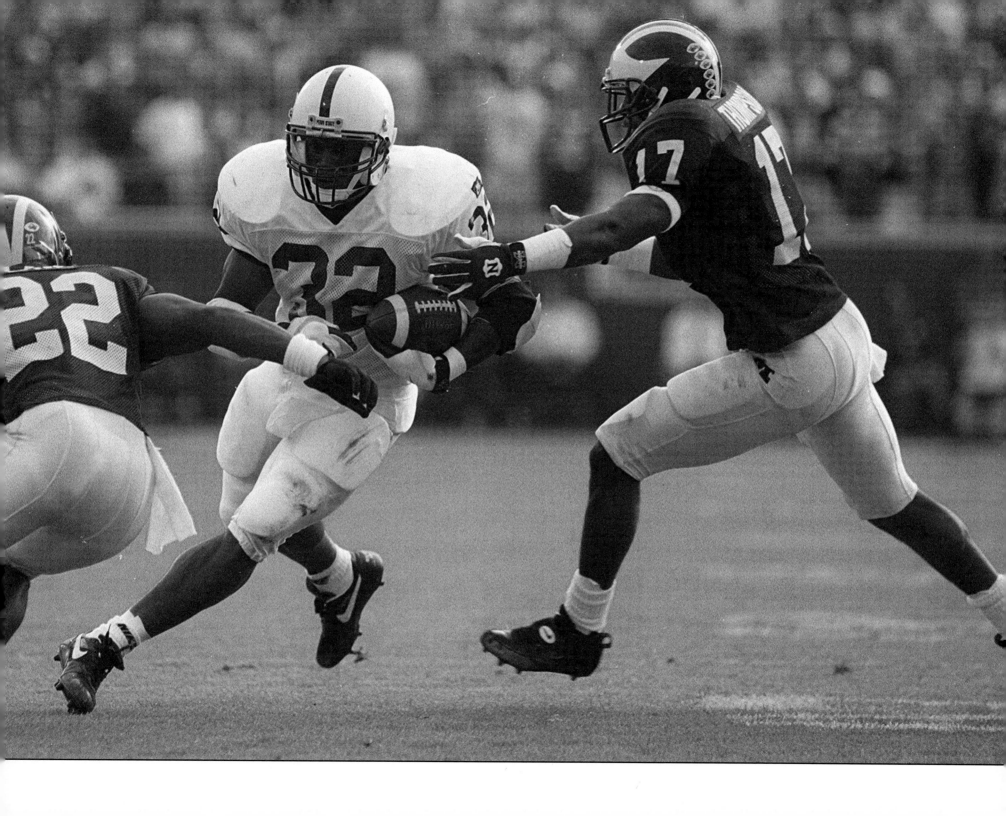

Penn State 63 Ohio State 14

October 29, 1994 | State College, Pa.

Lions Maul Ohio State in Big Ten Showdown

JOE
PATERNO
ERA

By Marino Parascenzo

Pittsburgh Post-Gazette

The Ohio State Buckeye's best defense today was a punt late in the first half. But this was a very special punt. The Buckeyes were fourth-and-10 at their own 40 and really hurting for points. But there was no way Coach John Cooper was going to turn the ball back over to Penn State this close, not even with a lousy 17 seconds left. You might go to halftime trailing by six touchdowns. So you punt. Better to go to halftime trailing by only five.

So the Nittany Lions finished the job in the second half, a 63-14 mauling that lifted their record to 7-0, kept them atop the Big Ten at 4-0, and possibly left them still No. 1 in the country, depending on how the pollsters assess No. 3 Nebraska's 24-7 win over No. 2 Colorado.

About rankings, Penn State coach Joe Paterno had this to say, grinning: "I don't have to talk about 'em, and I'm not gonna talk about 'em."

At any event, for a Beaver Stadium-record crowd of 97,079, the smell of the Rose Bowl got stronger. With Michigan losing to Wisconsin,

Ohio State	0	0	6	8 —	14
Penn State	7	28	14	14 —	63

Michigan, Ohio State and Illinois are all tied for a distant second in the Big Ten with 3-2 records.

"I don't see anybody beating them," Cooper said.

Was Paterno getting even for the Buckeyes' trash-talking win of last year? Or digging Ohio State President E. Gordon Gee for saying he had been outcoached? Or trying to nail down a national ranking he insists doesn't matter at the moment?

Paterno explained 'em all.

"I'm as surprised as anybody," he said. "They didn't have a good day, and we had a great day."

And a great team, Cooper allowed. "I just hope they're as great as I think they are," he added.

164

JOE
PATERNO
ERA

Kerry Collins (12) had little trouble with the Ohio State defense, completing 19 of 23 passes for 265 yards and two touchdowns.

Penn State tailback Ki-Jana Carter (32) opened the Lions' scoring in the first quarter.

At least this great:

■ Against Ohio State's fast-improving defense, No. 2 in the Big Ten, having allowed only 13.3 points per game, Penn State scored on four straight possessions in the second quarter.

■ Quarterback Kerry Collins, the nation's most efficient passer, redeemed a poor showing at Columbus last year with 19 for 23 passing for 265 yards and two touchdowns before coming out late in the third quarter. He hit receiver Bobby Engram and tailback Mike Archie for TD's, both from 15 yards.

■ Engram, not even a target until early in the second period, caught six passes for 102 yards, including a diving one-hander for 12 yards that set up Ki-Jana Carter's 36-yard TD run. Engram's 15-yard TD reception also was a diving catch. All of which made him happy.

"A lot of those guys were gloating and talking down to us last year," he said. "That's not right."

Ohio State defensive back Marlon Kerner, one of many badly burned in this game, shook his head. "I've been on teams that have won this big, but I've never lost a game like this," he said. "Not even in my wildest dreams did I think they'd scored 63 points on us."

Things got so bad for Ohio State that even Chris Maczyk scored for the Nittanies. He's a 279-pound defensive tackle, and he got his career-first TD when he intercepted quarterback Bobby Hoying's screen pass from the Ohio State 11. Crack receiver Joey Galloway — held to three catches for 31 yards — couldn't grab the towering lob, and it dropped in Maczyk's beefy hands. He turned like a startled rhino and lumbered 10 yards for the TD and a 56-6 lead.

Hoying was intercepted two other times, both by defensive back Brian Miller and both setting up TD's.

"I don't think we can play much better than we did in the first half," Paterno said. "The defense needs to get a little sharper for us to get to the next level."

Which leaves some to wonder what level he's talking about. The Lions gained 572 yards, (286 rushing and the same passing) to 214, had 33 first downs to 12 and logged four sacks to one.

Paterno praised Collins: "If there's a quarterback playing any better, he's got to be out of this world."

And Carter: "It's hard to imagine a better tailback in the country."

The Lions "plodded" through the first half. They scored on their first possession (for the fifth time this season), going 73 yards in eight plays, with Carter darting the final 20. But it took them three minutes and 12 seconds.

In the volcanic second quarter, Carter banged a yard for one TD (a glacial 5:34 drive), Engram made his diving TD catch (2:39), Carter blasted 36 yards (1:39) and Archie took his pass (0:35).

The Buckeyes took the ensuing kickoff, made one first down, then opted for the punt with 17 seconds left in the first half. They were

Ki-Jana Carter bowls over Ohio State's Tim Patillo (21) for some of the Nittany Lions' 572 yards of total offense.

already trailing, 35-0.

Cooper wasn't sure whether this was the most embarrassing loss of his career.

"But this was our first time out here," he said, "and we got embarrassed."

It could have been worse.

This was Ohio State's biggest loss since a 58-6 whipping by Michigan in 1946. But until they scored against the Penn State subs with about three minutes to play, it was looking like the worst loss since, oh, 1902 or thereabouts.

All of which created a new axiom — the longest distance between two points is the road back from State College to Columbus.

JOE PATERNO ERA

Bobby Engram caught six passes for 102 yards against the Ohio State defense.

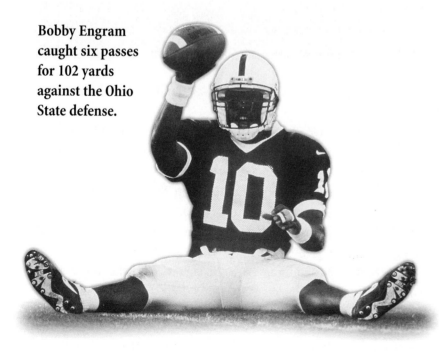

Penn State 38 Oregon 20

Lions Finish Season Unbeaten, but Uncrowned

By Marino Parascenzo

Pittsburgh Post-Gazette

Penn State	7	7	14	10 — 38
Oregon	7	0	7	6 — 20

Was this Rose Bowl the stuff of national championships?

Penn State's Nittany Lions say so, believing they staked their claim to at least a share of the national title today with a 38-20 victory over the Oregon Ducks in the Rose bowl.

Others might argue that Penn State's victory was an exercise in crisis survival.

The win left 102,247 fans hanging on the ropes. But for much of the game, the lightly regarded Ducks — 17-point underdogs — had the Lions hanging on the ropes.

In any event, if anything would have been enough to carry the No. 2 Penn State over No. 1 Nebraska and into the national championship, this game probably wasn't it. The final vote is due out tomorrow, and if the voters follow form, Nebraska, off a come-from-behind win over Miami in the Orange Bowl Sunday night, will keep its top ranking and win the mythical title. All of which was not being swallowed here tonight.

"We're going to award ourselves the national championship, no matter what the guys in their (easy) chairs say," said Penn State quarterback Kerry Collins.

"When a team gets inside the 20, Penn State plays really great defense," said Oregon's dynamite quarterback, Danny O'Neil, the co-Most Outstanding Player in the game. "That's why they're the national champs."

And Penn State running back Ki-Jana Carter, the other Most Outstanding Player: "The least they could do is split it up. We worked too hard not to get it."

Ki-Jana Carter scores in the third quarter to break a 14-14 tie with Oregon.

Brian Milne (22) bangs over from the 1-yard line for a Lions' TD.

Penn State was up by 38-14 on fullback Jon Witman's 9-yard run late in the fourth quarter. Oregon cut the score to its final margin of 18 points with Ricky Whittle's 3-yard run with 2:44 left in the game.

Penn State, the Big Ten champ, came in with an 11-0 record, ranked No. 2, and with the hottest offense in the land. Oregon, the Pacific-10 champ, was 9-3 and ranked No. 12, and was not expected to provide much more than an appetizer. The Ducks were a bone that got stuck in the Lions' throat. It was O'Neil who stuck it there.

O'Neil set Rose Bowl records with 41 completions in 61 passes for 456 yards. He also threw for two touchdowns and was intercepted twice, both times by Penn State junior free safety Chuck Penzenik, making the first start of his career.

Penzenik's second interception, late in the third quarter, set up Carter's third TD for the 28-14 lead. And when linebacker Terry Killens broke through and sacked O'Neil moments later, on the last play of the third period, the end was in sight.

The victory made Paterno the winningest bowl coach ever, with 16 victories, one more than the late

Carter scored three touchdowns. His first was an 83-yard bolt on Penn State's first play from scrimmage. He also scored from 17 and 3 yards, and had a game-high 156 yards on 21 carries.

Paterno chipped in, "We are worthy of being considered national champions like anyone else."

Passion and platitudes aside, if there is such a thing as a furious duck, that's what the Lions had to beat. The Ducks never led, but they tied the game twice. The Lions didn't begin to see daylight unitl late in the third quarter with 2:01 to play, in fact when Carter slammed in from 3 yards out for his final touchdown for a 28-14 lead.

Kerry Collins passed for 200 yards against the Ducks.

JOE PATERNO ERA

Paul (Bear) Bryant.

The Lions closed the season with a 12-0 record and a 17-game winning streak over two seasons. It was their first Rose Bowl win, in their second year in the Big Ten. They lost their first Rose Bowl, in 1923.

This one started out like another ho-hummer at Happy Valley. Oregon had to punt on the opening possession.

The Lions, accustomed to scoring in under two minutes, started at their own 17. This was over in a heartbeat. On the first play from scrimmage, Carter blasted through the right side, slammed over Herman O'Berry and raced 83 yards. This took 13 seconds. Penn State led, 7-0, with just under 11 minutes left in the first quarter.

And that's where the resemblance ended.

Now came the eerie echo from Paterno's pre-game warning, "If we're going to win this one, we're going to have to do it with good defense."

He was right, but he didn't have a good defense.

Oregon took the ensuing kickoff and O'Neil pounced on Penn State's defense like a pushy relative over the holidays. He just picked it apart like a Christmas goose. He hit tight end Josh Wilcox for 18 yards, tailback Dino Philyaw for 28, then Wilcox for 33 to the Lions' 1. And after a half-the-distance penalty, O'Neil finished off the dizzy Lions with a 1-yard flip to Wilcox for the TD and a 7-7 tie.

The Lions wedged ahead after Oregon kicker Matt Beldon, who blew a 23-yard field goal in the first quarter, then missed from 44 in the second.

Penn State accepted the invitation. Collins hit Bobby Engram for 18 yards, Engram again for 12, and later backup wide receiver Joe Jurevicius for 44 to the Oregon heartland. From there, Brian Milne hammered over from inches out at 1:26 of the second quarter, and Penn State was taking a 14-7 lead to intermission. But only after time ran out on Oregon. The devilish O'Neil drove the Ducks from their 18 to the Lions' 5 on an 8-for-8 passing drill that left the Lions giddy.

Paterno would need a nifty halftime talk. Something on the order of "Help!"

Whatever it was seemed to put some life and creativity into the Lions' defense for a while.

Soon, it was all over but the voting.

JOE PATERNO ERA

Joe Paterno points the way to victory.

171

Penn State 38 Oregon 20

September 12, f998 | State College, Pa.

Tears & Special Tales Flow With Paterno's 300th Win

By Joe Drape

The New York Times

JOE PATERNO ERA

| Bowling Green | 0 | 3 | 0 | 0 — | 3 |
| Penn State | 21 | 13 | 14 | 0 — | 48 |

He had dodged the questions about the milestones all week. He ducked one cooler full of water as time ticked down, but not a second cooler. Still, Joe Paterno did not really get wet until after more than 96,000 people reverently chanted his name. Until his wife, Sue, his five children and three grandchildren swarmed him at the 50-yard line.

Until he was presented with a portrait, and his players thrust their white helmets into the air to coax the fans in Beaver Stadium to roar again in one voice for him.

He took the microphone, and in a shaky voice began: "I'm so overwhelmed. I can't tell you how filled up with people, memories, all the years." Then the 71-year-old coach broke down and cried.

He has led Penn State football teams for 33 years and today, central Pennsylvania was not going to leave until the community of blue and white could savor 300 career victories with the man they call JoePa. "I have loved every moment," he said haltingly. "I have savored every effort of all my teams."

It was the most moving conclusion to a 48-3 rout. In walloping Bowling Green, a young Nittany Lions team helped Paterno reach a select group of 300 game-winners — a feat he achieved faster than the others. At 300-77-3 with a .793 winning percentage, Paterno joins Paul (Bear) Bryant (323), Pop Warner (319) and Amos Alonzo Stagg (314) in Division I-A, Eddie Robinson (408) in Division I-AA and John Gagliardi (343 and still coaching) in Division II, as record winners.

Not that the sold-out crowd of 96,291 minded, but Paterno's victory was ready for the record books just over one minute into the game.

In the Nittany Lions' first game, Cordell Mitchell took a handoff around the left end and did not stop until 77 yards later when he was in

172

Penn State's Cordell Mitchell (32) raced 74 yards for a first-quarter touchdown against Bowling Green.

Paterno was carried off the field by his players after his historic win.

the end zone.

It was the first of three consecutive single-play touchdown strikes that catapulted Penn State to a 21-0 first-quarter lead. Bruce Branch, a redshirt freshman, returned a punt 73 yards for a touchdown. Then the sophomore linebacker LaVar Arrington stepped in front of a pass by Falcons quarterback Bob Niemet and took it 16 yards for another score.

From there, the countdown to coaching history was delayed until Penn State was through punishing an overmatched Bowling Green.

His team's sterling performance was appreciated by Paterno.

He is fond of this year's squad, which has only six seniors and came into the season with just modest expectations.

"There were a lot of real good things that happened out there today," said Paterno, whose team outgained the Falcons 432 yards to 239. "We've got a chance to be a real tough team, though we're not there yet."

In turn, his team was moved by the emotion their coach showed after the game. More than a few had tears in their eyes as they listened to Paterno address the crowd. "It's amazing he's won that many," Arrington said. "Plus, Joe is special. He's allowed to get emotional."

Paterno has been voted coach of the year by his colleagues an unprecedented four times, and has won two national titles. Four times — in 1968, '69, '73 and '94 — his teams have gone undefeated but were denied the national title.

He has watched more than 200 of his Nittany Lions go to the National Football League. But before the game, members of Penn State's 1973 team — which was 12-0 and featured the Heisman Trophy winner John Cappelletti — wanted to talk about the man.

They shared beers and tales of their old coach.

They told each other how he became an institution in a way that transcended the wing of Penn State's library that is named after him.

"Joe always says you have to be a little kooky to be a coach, and he is," said Greg Buttle, the all-American linebacker and former New York Jet. "But what other coach can give you a dissertation about opera or mathematics, tell you about marriage and agents, or even take the time to want to talk to you.

"He never said you have to win the game. He just told us to play hard and have fun. He's an anomaly. He's a living legend who doesn't portray himself as one."

By the afternoon, Paterno indeed looked very human.

Red-eyed, with his 16-month-old grandson, Matthew, on his lap and the portrait of him and Sue to his left, he confessed that he felt the emotion of the day wash over him on a walk earlier in the morning when he began remembering games that had been long forgotten.

"I really didn't think this was that big a deal," he said. "I didn't think it would mean so much. But, gee, after the game it was tremendous," he said, his voice cracking again.

Then he remembered a story he told his team about the late H.L. Mencken.

"In Mencken's view," Paterno said, "there are two types of tales. One is the wonder of it and one is the shame of it. I want us to be the wonder of it."

And today, Paterno, the Nittany Lions and all of Happy Valley were.

JOE PATERNO ERA

175

PATERNO: A Renaissance Man and A Coach for the Ages

By Steve Halvonik

Pittsburgh Post-Gazette

As an outdoorsman, Joe Paterno falls somewhere between Marlin Fitzwater and Marlin Perkins.

He isn't into mountain-climbing or bird-watching, and his idea of a fishing trip is repairing to the back porch with a dogeared copy of *The Old Man and the Sea*.

But as he enters his stretch run at Penn State, Paterno has taken up a new hobby: big-game hunting.

He's loaded for Bear.

Paterno needs only 17 more wins to break the NCAA Division I-A record of 323 victories, set by the late Paul (Bear) Bryant of Alabama.

Paterno, who begins his 34th campaign with a record of 307-80-3, could have the record in five years if he maintains his current pace of 9-3 wins a season.

Paterno, who turned 70 in December 1996, says he would like to continue coaching five or so more years. But he denies he's gunning for Bryant.

"I'm not really interested in Bryant's record," Paterno insists. "I don't even think about it unless someone else brings it up. If it happens that I end up being here long enough to win more games than Bryant won, that would be great. But if it doesn't happen, it doesn't happen."

Paterno says his health will determine how long he remains in coaching.

"I don't have a timetable based on how many games I have to win," he says. "I have a timetable based on how effective I am. I could wake up two, three years from now and say I'm not up to this any more and get out of it."

If health is the determinant factor, then Paterno could be around well into the next millenium. He's the Dick Clark of coaches: He seems to get younger while everyone around him gets older.

Paterno is in excellent physical condition. His hair is dark and thick, his weight is down, and his mind is sharp as a cleat.

"I just saw Joe the other night and he looks younger than ever," former Penn State athletic director Jim Tarman marvels.

Tarman, who worked closely with Paterno for 35 years as sports information director and AD before retiring in 1993, says his old friend has never come right out and openly declared his interest in surpassing Bryant.

"But deep down inside," Tarman says, "I think Joe really wants to surpass Bear Bryant's record.

"It's not the only thing that's keeping him in coaching," Tarman adds. "I think he really likes working with young people and some of the things he's doing with the university. He likes power and all that comes with it. But deep down in, he really wants to pass Bear Bryant."

Paterno's expression of disinterest would go down easier if it were any other coach. But considering Bryant's towering stature, and Paterno's coaching relationship with him, you can't help but believe he would like to finish ahead of the Bear at least once in his lifetime.

Bryant, who led the Crimson Tide from 1958 to 1982, dominated college football like few other coaches before or since. He was 232-46-9 and won six national championships in Tuscaloosa. That includes a share of the 1978 title after a 14-7 Sugar Bowl win over Penn State that denied the Nittany Lions their first national crown.

Paterno has a deep and abiding admiration for Bryant as a coach. His voice drops almost to a church whisper as he recalls his first encounter with Bryant, at the 1959 Liberty Bowl.

"He was only in his second season at Alabama," Paterno says, "but he already had the reputation of becoming one of the game's great coaches. He had a very dominant personality."

Nevertheless, as Paterno discusses Bryant, he leaves the impression that they never made a love connection. Their relationship was strictly business, nothing personal, he seems to say.

What bugs Paterno is that for all his acclaim as a big-game coach,

At a crucial point in the game, Paterno attempts to signal-in his instructions to his squad.

Paterno argues with an official on the sidelines following a fight between Penn State and Pitt players in 1986.

JOE PATERNO ERA

he could never beat Bryant.

Paterno is 8-5-1 against Notre Dame, 6-4 against Miami (Fla.), 3-3 against Michigan and 3-2 against Southern Cal.

Yet is only 4-8 against Alabama, thanks to an 1-4 mark against Bryant.

Paterno readily admits that the New Year's Day 1979 Sugar Bowl defeat "was probably my toughest loss."

With less than two minutes remaining, Penn State failed to score on four cracks on the Alabama goal line.

"It got to me — it hammered at my ego," Paterno said of the loss in his autobiography, *Paterno: By the Book*. "When I stood toe to toe with Bear Bryant, he outcoached me."

Time has done little to relieve the pain. Paterno's face muscles still tense up as he reflects on that defeat.

"It was probably my toughest loss because I don't think I did a good job," he says. "People don't realize, but after that goal-line stand, we stopped them. They had to kick the ball and it went out of bounds. But we had 12 guys on the field and gave them a first down.

"We didn't give our kids a chance to win it. We could have won it."

Paterno also faults himself for not having himself or his team pre-

179

Born and raised in Brooklyn, N.Y., Paterno's successful coaching career and explosive personality has often been compared to another great Brooklyn native, Vince Lombardi.

pared for the hype and hoopla surrounding that game.

"When we got down there (to New Orleans), there were so many people, we couldn't get out of the hotel," Paterno says. "So we couldn't do the kind of job down there that we had to do to win the game, even though I thought we had the better personnel."

Even if he never breaks Bryant's record, Paterno will still be remembered as one of the game's legendary figures; the coach with the rolled-up pants and pop-bottle glasses who stood for something more than wins and losses.

Penn State's plain uniforms symbolize Paterno's philosophy of hard work, humility and personal sacrifice in the pursuit of team glory.

Paterno already ranks fourth in all-time wins, behind only Bryant, Glenn (Pop) Warner (319) and Amos Alonzo Stagg (314).

And he already holds the record for bowl victories, with 19, four more than Bryant.

His 34-year tenure at Penn State trails only Stagg's 41 at Chicago.

When he succeeded his mentor, Charles A. (Rip) Engle as head coach in 1966, after 16 years as an assistant, Penn State was little more than a run-of-the-mill, land-grant institution stuck in the middle of the Allegheny mountains. Today, it is generally recognized as one of the nation's premier public institutions.

Paterno deserves a big slice of the credit.

He owns the school's only two national championships, 19 of its 22 bowl wins, 21 of its 25 Lambert trophies (symbolic of Eastern football supremacy) and 40 percent of its 724 total victories. He's had only one losing season, has finished in the Top 10 19 times, and has coached undefeated teams in the 1960's, 70's, 80's and 90's.

Under his stewardship, Beaver Stadium has nearly doubled in size to nearly 94,000 seats, making it the second largest on-campus facility in the nation.

It's estimated that Penn State football generates as much as $40 million in busines for the Centre County economy.

Paterno's impact was underscored by a preseason magazine article that rated Penn State as the fifth-best football program of the 20th century, behind only Notre Dame, Alabama, Oklahoma and Nebraska. None of these other superpowers, it should be noted, has relied so much on one coach for its reputation as Penn State has on Paterno.

"Bear was the last living legend, and there is no question that Joe is there now," says former Nittany Lion Matt Millen.

Quite a tribute from a guy whom Paterno had once stripped of his captaincy.

If it's possible, Paterno has done even more for college football away from the field.

His "grand experiment," which emphasized the "student" in student-athlete, proved that universities could field successful teams without cutting academic corners or breaking NCAA rules.

"Joe's primary interest in his football players is as members of society," says Dr. Dave Joyner, an orthopedic surgeon and one of 22 first-team academic all-Americans Penn State has produced under Paterno. "He wanted you to be outstanding individuals in everything you did, not just as football players."

One reason the Big Ten Conference invited Penn State to join its league in 1989 was because of the university's reputation for both acad-

Paterno huddles with his wife, Sue, and daughters Mary Kathryn and Diana Lynne, after being named Penn State head football coach in 1966.

JOE PATERNO ERA

As a coach, Paterno has never been shy in expressing his views.

181

emic and athletic excellence — an image enhanced by Paterno.

Paterno, to be sure, has his detractors. Some of his coaching peers resent his pious image, and mockingly call him "St. Joe."

Over time, however, he has earned his colleagues' grudging respect.

In a poll published by Sports Illustrated last fall, 30 Division I-A coaches paid Paterno the ultimate compliment by picking him as the coach they would most want their son to play for.

Paterno has long captured the imagination of Penn State fans because of his intellectual restlessness and his indefatigable desire to making University Park a better place.

He loves talking military history with Indiana basketball coach Bob Knight. He is an unapologetic Republican — not because he is against affirmative action or welfare, but because of his deep conviction that government programs are a pale substitute for civic involvement.

Most of the time, though, Paterno is more pragmatist than ideologue.

He seconded George Bush for president at the 1988 Republican Convention, but his enthusiasm waned when Bush failed to keep his promise of being the "education president."

"Joe is more than a coach," Tarman says. "He has a very complicated, complex personality. He's very bright, very articulate. He has so many interests, and they're all woven into his coaching philosophy."

Befitting his Renaissance image, Paterno has donated his time to a myriad of university projects.

He helped spearhead a fund-raising drive that raised $350 million for the university in the 1980's. He and his wife, Sue, helped raise $14 million for the library, kicking in $250,000 out of their own pockets.

Paterno also helped raise money for the $55 million Bryce Jordan Center, and he personally donated another $250,000 for the construction of a $5 million university all-sports hall of fame.

One of the reasons Paterno cites for sticking around another five years is his desire to help Penn State successfully complete its next fund-raising campaign, a push for $1 billion—a goal which he has

Paterno and the Penn State team visit President Ronald Reagan in the White House in 1983 after winning the national title.

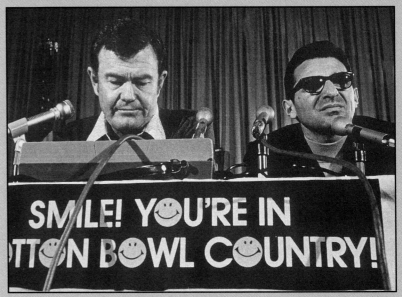

SMILE! YOU'RE IN
OTTON BOWL COUNTRY!

Paterno and Texas coach Darrell Royal answer questions from the media prior to the 1972 Cotton Bowl.